SECOND EDITION

ASSISTIVE TECHNOLOGY
IN SPECIAL EDUCATION

Resources for Education, Intervention, and Rehabilitation

Second Edition
Assistive Technology
in Special Education

Resources for Education, Intervention, and Rehabilitation

Joan L. Green

PRUFROCK PRESS INC.
WACO, TEXAS

Library of Congress Cataloging-in-Publication Data

Green, Joan L., 1963-
 Assistive technology in special education : resources for education, intervention, and rehabilitation / by Joan L. Green. -- Second edition.
    pages cm.
 Includes bibliographical references.
 ISBN 978-1-61821-084-5 (pbk.)
 1. Communication devices for people with disabilities. 2. Assistive computer technology. 3. Self-help devices for people with disabilities. 4. Special education--Technological innovations. 5. Educational technology. I. Title.
 HV1568.G74 2013
 371.9'045--dc23
                                       2013025369

Prufrock Press Inc.
P.O. Box 8813
Waco, TX 76714-8813
Phone: (800) 998-2208
Fax: (800) 240-0333
http://www.prufrock.com

TABLE OF CONTENTS

Acknowledgements vii

A Note to the Reader. ix

Chapter 1   *The Power of Technology.* 1

Chapter 2   *The Benefits of Assistive Technology* 5

Chapter 3   *Technologies and Access* 11

Chapter 4   *Technology and Strategies to Improve Verbal Expression* . . 25

Chapter 5   *Augmentative and Alternative Communication:*
             Devices, Apps, and More 59

Chapter 6   *Technology and Strategies to Improve*
             Auditory Comprehension 75

Chapter 7   *Technology and Strategies to Improve*
             Reading Comprehension. 87

Chapter 8   *Drill-and-Practice Technology to Improve Reading Skills* 109

Chapter 9   *Technology and Strategies to Improve Written Expression* 125

Chapter 10   *Drill-and-Practice Technology to Improve Writing Skills.* 151

Chapter 11   *Technology and Strategies to Improve Executive*
             Function and New Learning 161

Chapter 12   *Interactive Programs to Improve Cognition,*
             Learning, and Memory 191

Chapter 13   *Interactive Websites and Games to Promote*
             Communication, Literacy, and Learning. 213

Chapter 14   *Helpful Online Resources and Learning Tools* 221

References 229

About the Author 231

Index 233

ACKNOWLEDGEMENTS

· · · · · · · · · · · ·

I am grateful to:

- my husband, Mark Green, for his continuous love and support during this project;
- my children, Hallie, Ilana, Elise, and Aaron, for their encouragement and helping me explore some of the technologies that teenagers and students use daily;
- my parents, Allan and Leah Lipman, and my brother, Bob Lipman, for their enthusiasm and for always supporting my efforts;
- the many client and families I have had the pleasure of working with who have put their faith in me to help them;
- many colleagues who share my passion for using technologies to help people with disabilities and devote their professional lives to producing technologies or sharing their knowledge about assistive technologies that can be used to improve so many lives; and
- our new puppy, Teddie, who has kept our family very busy, but happy, as we miss Honey, our yellow lab who passed away a few months ago.

A NOTE TO THE READER

. . . .

I was very pleased when I was informed that the first edition of this book was a top seller and was asked to write an updated version, although many people warned me against trying to write a book about assistive technology because products and features change so fast. I agree that it is challenging to capture the best tools and record them in a book, but I believe that many people still want to hold a book in their hands for guidance on this topic. What I hadn't anticipated was the amount of work and time this update would require. It's incredible how much has changed in just a couple of years! We are in the midst of an exciting shift in the many ways technology can help people with disabilities. There are bound to be many bumps in this process and it is hard for everyone to stay on top of the changes, but well worth the effort.

Please use the resources presented in this guide as a starting point from which to learn more. The information should not be used to replace professional consultations and services. This guide is not intended to prescribe evaluation or treatment protocols for students. Skilled intervention is needed for students who struggle to communicate, read, write, and learn. Anyone who decides to integrate technology into education and remediation must expect to invest time and effort into exploring and trying the resources to learn which are best for their situation. In my private speech therapy practice, when I provide therapy, I use many strategies and approaches that do not involve technology. Although this book is primarily focused on technology tools, skilled therapists and teachers need to keep in mind that technology does not replace their areas of expertise. Tools do not replace people, they can just be very helpful when used effectively.

If you would like to continue to receive guidance from me on what I perceive to be top picks for technologies to help students, please subscribe to my free e-newsletter at http://www.innovativespeech.com. I try to send out information about twice a month. It is in that e-mail that I also post information about upcoming workshops and webinars as well as additional online resources as they are posted on my website. Feel free to e-mail me at Joan@innovativespeech.com or call 301-602-2899 or 1-800-IST-2550 if you would like to discuss your situation and how I might be able to help you.

CHAPTER 1

THE POWER OF TECHNOLOGY

CUTTING-EDGE TECHNOLOGY OFFERS NEW HOPE

As the affordability and availability of fantastic new multimedia tools that promote personal, academic, and vocational success and independence increase, so does the potential for greater success for people who have communication, learning, and cognitive challenges. Teachers, therapists, and families need to embrace these tools and learn to adapt these cutting-edge technologies to empower individuals with literacy, learning, and communication differences. Unfortunately, many of the people who could benefit the most from these recent advances remain in paper-based worlds—receiving services that do not take advantage of effective new technology tools. Many individuals with disabilities are often never exposed to new affordable products that can help them succeed in life. As our society becomes increasingly dependent on technologies for communication and information access, people with disabilities are experiencing an ever-increasing digital divide. Everyone deserves to be exposed to mainstream as well as specialized, easy-to-use resources with which they can accomplish everyday tasks with increased ease and efficiency. The world of technology has become much more affordable—many state-of-the-art resources are now readily available and when used properly, can have a huge positive impact on the lives of individuals with autism, learning differences, communication challenges, cognitive deficits, and developmental disabilities.

ASSISTIVE TECHNOLOGY

Assistive technology devices (also referred to as adaptive technology) refer to any "item, piece of equipment, or product system, whether acquired commercially, modified, or customized, that is used to increase, maintain, or improve functional capabilities of individuals with disabilities" (Assistive Technology Act of 2004, § 3.4). Assistive technologies can remove barriers to independence and success, especially when used in the individual's natural setting such as his or her home, school, or workplace. These tools can reduce the burden of difficult skills and enhance independence during daily life at school, work, home, and in the community.

HELPFUL TECHNOLOGIES ARE ALL AROUND US

The worlds of assistive technology (AT), educational technology, and mainstream technology are merging. Change is happening so fast that it is difficult to stay on top of the many new ways technology can be used to help people of all ages who have subtle or debilitating challenges. This guide will introduce you to an exciting world of assistive technology—one that includes many products and approaches which you may not know exist, as well as many you may be very familiar with but have not thought to use to help improve speaking, reading, writing, listening, thinking, memory, or learning.

TAKING THE FIRST STEP

Whether you are a parent of a child with communication, learning, or attention challenges, a teacher or therapist trying to offer the best help you can for those to whom you provide services, or an older student exploring this topic on your own, the keys to success in using this guide are the same:

- Start gradually.
- Focus on the sections within chapters that will meet your immediate needs first.
- Start to network with others in similar situations by joining online support and discussion groups.
- Explore the websites of products that seem relevant to your situation to make sure that you learn about the most recent specifications, features, and price of the products.
- Try out the many free resources and online sources for support that may help.
- Be creative and try new things. There is no one correct way to proceed.

SEEK PROFESSIONAL GUIDANCE

This book does not replace the need for skilled professional intervention. Although assistive technologies are helpful in the education and therapy process, they do not replace specialized help from trained educators and therapists. Users of the technology need to remain focused on their goals and work to achieve the desired outcomes. Once a good match with the user and product is made, the selected resource should be configured or used in the best way to maximize progress toward goals. Some activities may be enjoyable, but aren't effective toward learning new skills. People learn in different ways and are helped by different strategies and types of assistance. Communication and cognitive professionals such as speech-language pathologists are trained to help people with communication and cognitive deficits, and computers are only tools to further that help. One product can be used in many ways. Figuring out the most effective way to use the technology is critical for success. Also, it is important to keep in mind that the latest cool tools aren't always the best. Many years of research have been devoted to this field of assistive technology and some of the dedicated communication systems and products that have been available for a long time may be better than newer products developed for mobile technologies. There are pros and cons to most products and the key is figuring out the best fit for your particular situation.

TAKE ADVANTAGE OF PRODUCT SUPPORT AND ONLINE REVIEWS AND VIDEOS

Once you select software, adaptive hardware, mobile devices, or suggested websites that are potentially helpful for you in your setting, spend some time exploring the websites that are given for the products discussed or search online for reviews or video tutorials. If you go to a search engine such as Bing or Google and enter the name of the product and the word "reviews," you can often see what others have said about the product. Bloggers and review sites are often very helpful. Be careful, however, about giving too much credibility to one disgruntled user who leaves a bad review. It's hard to know the true reason that they had a bad experience. YouTube (http://www.youtube.com) also often has helpful videos to watch. Many businesses offer free trials via download. Other helpful features offered by some companies are the ability to join an electronic mailing list, participate in chat sessions, receive free e-newsletters, or access a bulletin board that will connect you to other users of the product.

BEST SOLUTIONS

I frequently get asked the following types of questions:

- What is the best tablet to use for my son with dyslexia?
- What should I try if my daughter is 3 and hasn't started talking yet?
- My child is very disorganized and about to start his first year in college. Which technologies are best for him?

Successful solutions require careful thought as well as trial and error. So much depends on the individual student and the situation. The best solutions are those that work effectively to help the student accomplish a set of goals. There is no "one size fits all" fix for a problem. It's imperative to keep in mind that technologies are just tools that can be used to assist in the education and intervention process.

I have done my best to include helpful online resources throughout this guide. I also repeat important concepts for individuals who may choose to read only a chapter or two. Here are a few of my top picks for learning more about using technologies to help students with special needs. I have scattered more top picks for online resources in other chapters.

TOP PICKS FOR LEARNING
ABOUT TECHNOLOGIES

- **Kathy Schrock's Guide to Everything** (http://www.schrockguide.net/app-for-that.html)
- **Karen Janowski's Free Technology Toolkit for UDL in All Classrooms** (http://udltechtoolkit.wikispaces.com)
- **Lauren Enders' Pinterest** (http://pinterest.com/lasenders)— Please take a look at her boards featuring Android resources. I have much more experience with Apple devices, so those of you with Android devices don't want to miss her Android Apps for Special Education (http://pinterest.com/lasenders/android-apps-for-special-education), Speech Apps for Android Devices (http://pinterest.com/lasenders/speech-apps-for-android-devices), and Language Apps for Android Devices (http://pinterest.com/lasenders/language-apps-for-android-devices).

CHAPTER 2

THE BENEFITS OF ASSISTIVE TECHNOLOGY

WE NEED TO EMBRACE THE USE OF ASSISTIVE TECHNOLOGY TO HELP THOSE IN NEED

Technology has slowly crept into our lives. Assistive technology has become an integral part of this evolution and is gaining increased acceptance in the delivery of services in school, therapy practices, and rehabilitation centers. Some professionals have welcomed this development of new resources to help others with open arms; some have avoided, resisted, or ignored these helpful tools; and others are unaware that new and exciting treatment opportunities exist.

Schools, healthcare systems, and vocational settings are struggling to balance the delivery of quality services with increasing costs and regulations. With the use of the assistive technologies highlighted in this guide, we become empowered to revolutionize the ability to contain costs, adhere to stringent regulations, and effectively help people of all ages with a wide range of communication, learning, and cognitive challenges. The key is to make a good match between the individual and the technology being used.

As technology continues to become more powerful, less expensive, and more portable, it becomes increasingly helpful in improving speaking, understanding, reading, writing, new learning, reasoning, and remembering. By creating opportunities as well as removing performance barriers, technology can help us explore new frontiers.

TECHNOLOGY IS EVERYWHERE!

The use of computers in education and therapy first appeared in the late 1970s with the advent of microcomputers. Word processors gradually replaced typewriters. In the 1980s, computer use in education and therapy progressed to the use of drill-and-practice exercises with instant feedback to facilitate the learning process. The 1990s ushered in easier access to the Internet and more sophisticated software programs with voice output, the ability to customize options in programs for users, and more interesting and interactive software. Treatment started to incorporate the use of e-mail and websites for reading practice, research, and promotion of self-advocacy. Technology has continued to become more sophisticated and affordable. More and more people have high-speed Internet access, cloud-based services such as iCloud, Evernote, and Dropbox, and computers as well as mobile technologies at home. Many students also have cell phones with texting and Internet access, tablets, social networking accounts, and are computer savvy.

We are now in the midst of another technology transformation and need to change our mindset. The world of Web 2.0 has been around for a while with its emphasis on information sharing and collaboration. There is now a growing emphasis on using products that are helpful to everyone. There is a push toward a universal design for learning (UDL), created by the Center for Applied Special Technology (CAST; http://www.cast.org). UDL provides a "blueprint for creating flexible goals, methods, materials, and assessments that accommodate learner differences" (Kurzweil Education Systems, n.d., p. 1). In the world of assistive technology, there is also now more of an emphasis on helping teachers learn to modify instruction and helping students find alternate methods to demonstrate what they know.

In schools there is an effort being made to create benchmark performance levels across the states with Common Core State Standards (CCSS). Technology is an integral part of this process. More information can be found at the CCSS website (http://www.corestandards.org).

DISABILITIES HINDER AN INDIVIDUAL'S ABILITY TO BENEFIT FROM MAINSTREAM TECHNOLOGY USE

Communication and cognitive deficits create obstacles to the use of technology that is becoming increasingly important in mainstream society.

It may be difficult for individuals with communication and cognitive challenges to:

- provide computer input with movement of a mouse or by typing on the keyboard,
- use a small mobile device,
- read and interpret information on the screen,
- sequence and analyze procedures needed to use software applications,
- use e-mail to obtain information and interact socially, and/or
- search online for information.

ASSISTIVE TECHNOLOGY OFFERS MANY BENEFITS

Appropriately selected assistive technologies can

- save time;
- motivate and engage the user;
- make tasks easier and more enjoyable;
- have real-life value;
- support unique learning styles, abilities, and backgrounds;
- provide feature flexibility and customizability at a level previously impossible;
- facilitate positive outcomes by carefully controlling tasks;
- give independent, nonjudgmental, immediate feedback;
- promote effective independent practice;
- streamline data and information collection;
- enable users to create, store, and access documents and resources from multiple locations;
- provide opportunities to document change over time objectively;
- increase opportunities for socialization and reduce isolation;
- enhance lifelong learning;
- provide more effective studying and learning strategies; and
- empower users to collaborate online.

MANY DIFFERENT TYPES OF PEOPLE CAN BENEFIT FROM ASSISTIVE TECHNOLOGY

Many new devices, software programs, and applications have been developed to help people confronted with a wide variety of challenges. People who are appropriate candidates for learning support from technology may have the following:

- developmental delay;

- attention issues;
- autism;
- executive functioning challenges (scheduling, planning, following through);
- reading and writing deficits (dyslexia, dysgraphia, arthritis, vision issues);
- learning disabilities;
- social, emotional, and behavioral challenges;
- developmental apraxia of speech;
- intellectual and cognitive impairments;
- poor performance in school;
- work-related challenges;
- unintelligible speech (dysarthria);
- dysfluent speech (stuttering);
- difficulty learning English as a second language;
- a voice disorder;
- hearing impairment;
- low vision;
- lack of interest or motivation in school-related activities;
- head injury (tumors, ruptured aneurysm, concussion, traumatic brain injury, gunshot wound);
- seizure disorder; or
- social thinking challenges.

FAMILY ADVOCACY PUSHES PROFESSIONALS TO LEARN ABOUT AVAILABLE RESOURCES

Often the family members of students with disabilities take the initiative to learn more about educational methods and treatment options. They expect their teachers and therapists to use state-of-the-art tools and methods, but teachers and therapists often don't have the luxury of time and effective training to support this transition. Parents confront their child's struggles every day and are very motivated to seek alternative solutions to maximize school success and self-esteem. Teachers and administrators want to do their best to help each student access the curriculum but confront many challenges when implementing assistive technologies and mobile solutions. It is an enormous challenge to integrate new technologies into a system that is already confronted with many regulations and challenges. This is a time of enormous conflict between families wanting to offer their child the newest and what they perceive to be the best assistive technology tools and schools that have a limited budget and limited tech-savvy personnel.

This guide streamlines the learning process and hopefully will make it less daunting for families, therapists, teachers, and other professionals to learn about ways to help students who struggle academically. Families, educators, and clinicians who are willing to collaborate and explore what these new tools can do in solution-focused sessions to supplement other techniques can achieve excellent results. Incorporating affordable technology into education and vocational training is well worth the effort, time, motivation, and dedication it requires. This guide highlights software, hardware, and other resources that are versatile and therapeutically and educationally beneficial.

TECHNOLOGY ADVANCES CONTINUE

The items included in this guide are not an exhaustive list of instructional tools and strategies, but rather a representative sampling of products available on the market and some suggestions about how to use them. It is inevitable that more products will become available and items described will change. New and improved features of software and apps are made available on a daily basis. Use the information included in this book as a guide for learning more about how assistive technology can help you in your situation.

SOFTWARE AND APPS CAN QUICKLY PROVIDE COMPENSATORY STRATEGIES TO GREATLY IMPROVE A VARIETY OF ABILITIES

Some of the compensatory strategies that software can provide include the following:

- Text-to-speech accessibility options, software, and apps can provide instant support for individuals who have good auditory comprehension skills but poor reading comprehension or visual-perceptual deficits. Digital text can be read aloud, highlighted, and enlarged to improve reading comprehension and retention. Students may then be able to better understand a school assignment, read e-mail from a friend, or scan an assignment and have the text read aloud.
- Voice-recognition software can help those who have difficulty writing. It enables individuals with relatively clear speech and intact cognition to talk and have the computer, tablet, or smartphone type what they say.

- Graphic organizers can help people who have difficulty thinking of words and organizing written narrative by providing a means for them to brainstorm and represent their thoughts with images and visual support. There are products that are used and saved on a device or others that enable the user to work online in the "cloud."
- Word prediction technology and online dictionaries are helpful for people who have difficulty thinking of words. Several products offer semantic linking so that a person who can't think of a word can type in a related word and gradually click on items to help find the word they were trying to type or say.
- Digital calendars and organizers can help people who have problems keeping track of daily activities and have poor time management skills. These programs can be on a computer, online, or on a mobile device.
- A digital pen can record audio as a person writes, to assist with recall of a lecture for a student who has trouble taking notes in class or to provide talking flash cards.
- Communication software and apps can empower people who can't speak by selecting pictures or words and having the device speak for them. Many of these products can be customized to meet the needs of the user and many offer a "dynamic display" so that people can zero in on what they are trying to communicate with a couple of clicks.

CHAPTER 3

TECHNOLOGIES AND ACCESS

HELPFUL PRODUCTS ARE BECOMING LESS EXPENSIVE

Technology can provide a new world of independence for students with physical, communication, or cognitive disabilities. Designing environments, products, and information to be easily used by the greatest number of people, with or without disabilities, has become much more prevalent in the development of technological products. This translates into mainstream technology that is more accessible and serves the different needs and personal preferences of many users, including people with communication, learning, and cognitive deficits. Many hardware options and mainstream products are available with accessibility features and can be modified to provide workable solutions for users with disabilities. A product created for mainstream society may be the perfect assistive technology device for a student who struggles with reading and writing.

EASE OF ACCESS

One of the first steps when using technology is to determine which method of access is the most appropriate. For individuals with physical and cognitive limitations, it is often difficult to use computers, tablets, and cell phones with the same ease as the rest of society. They may have difficulty with vision, dexterity, language, or learning new procedures. It is often important to try a variety of devices, screens, monitors, keyboards, styluses, mice, gestures, and switches to determine the best access method for that person. I always encourage professionals as well as family members to explore the accessibility features and options of devices, apps, and software, as well as peripherals such as keyboards and switches, in order to help make the best match of the person's needs with available technologies.

Easy-to-implement accessibility features are much more mainstream now than in the past, and very helpful features are often includes for free. Text can be read aloud and enlarged for free on many computers, tablets, smartphones, and browsers. People with clear speech can speak and have words typed automatically. More of these features are discussed throughout this guide.

When an individual has multiple physical issues and may benefit from help with positioning, adapted switches, or other complex access issues, a multidisciplinary assistive technology team is ideal to establish the best method of computer access. A comprehensive evaluation should be performed with input from the members of an educational, rehabilitation, or vocational team. Once the individual has the appropriate setup, a strategy can be developed for the use of technology to improve and compensate for communication, cognitive, literacy, and community-based challenges.

GUIDANCE FOR COMPUTER ACCESS AND ASSISTIVE TECHNOLOGIES

Several products and a number of extremely helpful online articles and protocols are available to assist with determining the most appropriate way for an individual to access technology.

The SETT Framework: Critical Areas To Consider When Making Informed Assistive Technology Decisions
by Joy Zabala
http://www.joyzabala.com

- The SETT Framework is a free tool that helps guide the decision-making process for technology by focusing the decision makers on the student, the environment, the tasks, and the tools. It was produced to assist teams through a variety of activities needed to help students select, acquire, and use assistive technology devices and software.

WATI (The Wisconsin Assistive Technology Initiative)

http://www.wati.org

- There are a number of very helpful free resources to print under the "Supports" tab. An entire guide titled "Assessing Students' Needs for Assistive Technology (ASNAT) 5th Edition" is available for download. Each chapter can be accessed as a PDF file, in Microsoft Word, or in PowerPoint. Helpful chapters that are available include AT for Communication; AT for Computer Access; AT for Writing, Including Motor Aspects; AT for Composition of Written Material; AT for Reading; and AT for Organization.

Compass Access Assessment Software

by Koester Performance Research (KRP)

http://www.kpronline.com

- This software measures the user's skills during eight skill tests using three input processes on a computer: pointing, text entry, and switch use to record data on the speed and accuracy of performance.
- Mac and Windows
- $179

MOBILE APPS

ATEval2Go

by Smarty Ears

- This app provides a guide and template to help evaluators document observations and considerations for AT during the evaluation process.
- iOS
- $39.99

AAC Evaluation Genie

by Hump Software

- This is an informal tool to help the speech-language pathologist and others identify appropriate visual stimuli and language representations for communication tools.
- iOS
- $9.99

SWITCH SOFTWARE

Some individuals with significant motor impairments need to obtain access to the computer or mobile devices with the use of switches and scanning. They may be unable to use a hand to touch a screen or use a mouse or trackball. As long as a person is able to reliably move one part of the body, they can utilize technologies that offer special access methods. Foot, shoulder, or head movement and even eye gaze can be used to access technology. There are many types of access solutions available with a wide range of price points and features. Matching the right access technology to the abilities of the individual is incredibly important and professional help should be used.

Options exist for users who use a single switch to operate computer software and mobile device apps. A single switch can be used to simulate mouse function or touch for a touch screen. People can also use multiple switches, giving access to more controls. Switch-friendly software programs offer special onscreen layouts with several choices. Users then use the switch to select desired choices when a highlighted box moves over items on the screen one after the other, until the student presses the switch to make a selection. This process is referred to as switch scanning.

The process of scanning involves many skills, such as controlling the switch, paying attention to the pictures or sounds on the screen, and watching what happens after the selection is made. Mounting of the switch, body positioning, and switch selection and setup all have to be considered. When an individual is only able to access software via a single switch, software and app selection is more limited. Many of the products described in this guide are accessible for people who need to use a switch. More detailed guidance on the use of technology and potential software for these users can be found at the following websites:

- **Switch in Time:** http://www.switchintime.com—This website has quite a few free programs for both Mac and Windows platforms.
- **Judy Lynn Software:** http://www.judylynn.com—Judy Lynn produces a variety of switch software for computers and mobile devices as well as helpful guidance for people with special needs.
- **Don Johnston:** http://www.donjohnston.com—This site offers a variety of switch-accessibile software available for purchase. Type "switch" in their search box.
- **HelpKidzLearn:** http://www.helpkidzlearn.com—This is a collection of online games and iOS as well as Android apps that are switch accessible. They also sell a switch interface and wireless switch bundle.

- **Hiyah.net:** http://www.hiyah.net—This free software has a full variety of switch activities for learners with multiple or significant special needs.
- **Northern Grid:** http://www.northerngrid.org/resource/sen-switcher—SENSwitcher is a suite of free programs designed to help teach early skills to people with profound and multiple learning difficulties, those who need to develop skills with assistive input devices, and very young children new to computers.
- **RJ Cooper & Associates:** http://www.rjcooper.com—This company has developed a number of switches for computers as well as mobile devices. Type "switch" in the search box.
- **Shiny Learning:** http://www.shinylearning.co.uk—Products here can be accessed using a variety of input devices such as switches, keyboard, or mouse.

COMPUTER OPERATING SYSTEMS AND THE DEVICES THEY RUN

As time passes, computers improve, helpful features become more mainstream, and costs decrease. Even the least expensive new computers are typically more than adequate and may actually be better than top-of-the-line products available just a few years ago. New complex software products with voice recognition or video do sometimes require significant amounts of memory and often function better with higher speed computers. Specific requirements for particular products are listed on their websites.

New types of computers are always being developed. The latest iterations offer some features that are helpful for students with communication and cognitive challenges. Some of these newer features include:

- laptops that are slimmer and lighter with fast performance,
- faster boot times and longer battery lives,
- products with built-in apps with assistive features for reading and writing,
- "convertible" computers with touch screens and tablets with keyboard docks, and
- the ability to use voice recognition (user speaks and computer writes) and record audio as users type.

Examples of computers that include these features are:
- **MacBook Air** (http://www.apple.com/macbook-air)

- **HP EliteBook** (http://www8.hp.com/us/en/ads/elite-products/products.html#books)
- **Google's Samsung Chromebook** (http://www.google.com/chromebook)
- **Lenovo ThinkPad Convertible Tablet** (http://shop.lenovo.com/us/en/laptops/thinkpad/x-series/x1-carbon-touch/?iPromoID=bannerX1Touch&)

It is important to understand the advantages and disadvantages of desktop computers, laptop and convertible computers, tablets, and other devices when deciding what to use. It can be helpful to consult with computer-savvy friends and colleagues when determining which type of technology to purchase. Also, be sure to take a look at the many online resources when deciding how to move forward. There are many blogs, podcasts, e-newsletters, and other helpful tools to learn more about assistive technology. Many are listed throughout this guide or can be found through an online search. It's important to connect with others in similar situations for guidance and to be able to try products before investing a significant amount of money in them. Computer magazine reviews, such as those in *PC Magazine* (http://www.pcmag.com) and *Consumer Reports* (http://www.consumerreports.org), are often also insightful for reviewing mainstream technologies.

OPERATING SYSTEMS AND DEVICES

An operating system is the software on a device that manages the programs and determines what can be done by the user. It is very important to know what assistive technology you will want to use when deciding which device to purchase in order to make sure that they are compatible.

- **PCs (Personal Computers):** When people use the term PC they are typically referring to a Windows-based computer. Microsoft Windows is the most common operating system for PCs and has changed over the years—Windows XP, Vista, Windows 7, and now Windows 8, which was released in October 2012. Windows 8 can be used on desktops, laptops, and tablets. In this guide, I generally write PC for software products that can be used with the Windows operating system. The Microsoft website (www.microsoft.com/enable/training/windows8) offers a collection of video demos for Windows 8 accessibility features including the touch screen, speech to text and text to speech, magnification, and how to customize the computer.

- **Open Source:** There are also open-source computer platforms that can be used on PCs such as Linux and Ubuntu. These platforms are available for anyone to use, modify, and redistribute freely.
- **Mac OS:** Apple computers such as the iMac and MacBook Air are very popular but tend to be more expensive than PCs. The operating systems have changed over the years and until now their names have had a cat theme. Some of the laptop and desktop operating systems included the Cheetah, Jaguar, Tiger, Leopard, Snow Leopard, Lion, and Mountain Lion. The company is breaking from this tradition with a new operating system named "Mavericks."
- **Tablets and Smartphones:** The production of a variety of tablets and smartphones has soared in recent years and there are now many options available. I believe that the iPad is currently the best way to go for individuals with special needs. There are very helpful accessibility features and many more apps geared to helping students with communication, literacy, and cognitive challenges. However, Android and Windows products are gaining in popularity due to their lower cost, and many developers who started developing apps for the iDevices are now starting to produce apps for tablets using other operating systems.
- **iOS:** This is the operating system used by iPhones and iPads; iOS 7 is the most recent version. It offers wonderful accessibility features that are very helpful for students with special needs, including guided access, speak selection with highlighting, voice to text, and zoom features.
- **iPads:** There have been six iterations of the iPad. The earliest version did not include built-in cameras and the latest accessibility features. There are currently two versions being sold, the iPad with Retina Display and the mini iPad. Size is the only significant difference. Each can be purchased with different amounts of memory, but are able to run the same apps. All apps made for an iPhone can be used on an iPad. Some will automatically adjust to the larger screen; others need to be magnified by selecting the 2x at the bottom of the screen. Not all iPad apps can work on an iPhone; some require the dimensions of the larger screen. Some new apps will only run on newer iPads.
- **iPhones:** The first generation iPhone was released in 2007. Just about every year a new version has been released. Most, but not all, apps made for the iPad can work on the iPhone.
- **Android:** The Android operating system powers all Android devices. It is an open-source system; many developers contribute

and develop their own systems using it. Google is the overseeing company. Manufacturers of mobile devices such as the Kindle Fire or Galaxy Pro tablet can modify the Android operating system as they see fit for their devices. This results in changes for the requirements of apps to run on the devices. Therefore, when determining whether or not you are able to use an Android app on an Android device, you need to be sure to know if it is compatible. In order to find out, it may be necessary to go to the app store affiliated with your particular device and check it out. There have been quite a few versions of the Android operating system. The first Android phone was sold in 2008. Since then, the operating systems have been referred to as Cupcake, Donut, Eclair, Froyo, Gingerbread, Honeycomb, Ice Cream Sandwich, and Jelly Bean.

APPLE COMPUTERS/DEVICES

Apple includes assistive technology in its products as standard features. Macintosh computers and iOS mobile devices offer many built-in accessibility features. Apple refers to these features collectively as Universal Access. More information can be found at http://www.apple.com/accessibility.

PERSONAL COMPUTERS/MICROSOFT

Windows 8 is the current platform, but individuals are still using many prior versions. Details and tutorials about its accessibility options can be found at http://www.microsoft.com/enable. All of the platforms offer built-in accessibility settings and programs that make it easier for computer users to see, hear, and use their computers.

The Ease of Access Center is a central location that you can use to set up the accessibility settings and programs available in Windows. You'll also find a link to a questionnaire that Windows can use to help suggest settings that you might find useful.

To open the Ease of Access Center, click the Start button, click Control Panel, and then click Ease of Access.

COMPUTER FORMAT—DESKTOPS, LAPTOPS, MOBILE DEVICES, AND HYBRIDS

The many different technology formats each have pros and cons. Most are now available with integrated touch screens, wireless Internet access (wifi), Bluetooth, and the capacity to accommodate adapted keyboards and other alternate input devices.

During the selection process, it is necessary to consider:

- the degree of mobility needed,
- the compatibility with apps and software,
- the cost,
- the level of support that will be provided,
- the need for online access, and
- most importantly, the needs of the user and tasks that will be required.

DESKTOPS

Desktop computers are the most versatile, offer the largest monitor and keyboard, can accommodate a wide range of assistive technologies, and often provide the greatest value for equivalent specifications. Desktops are typically used when there is one designated computer location, and when the user wants to use a computer for more than simple word processing and Internet use. They are more difficult to transport. Newer, upscale versions offer integrated touch screens and the central processing unit integrated into the monitor, which is more convenient for changing locations.

LAPTOPS

Laptop computers offer all of the functionality of desktop computers. Compared to a desktop alternative, they are easier to transport and store, but the monitor and integrated keyboards are typically smaller.

When compared to tablets and handheld devices, their weight prevents them from being easily transported. They generally have longer initial startup times and often have shorter battery lives. The keyboards are smaller than those of desktops, which may make them difficult to use for people who have visual or manual dexterity issues.

Accommodations can make laptop computers easier to use. Larger or adapted keyboards can be attached by USB port or wirelessly using Bluetooth, alternate mice and trackballs can be used, and talking software can read aloud text shown on the monitor.

An advantage of this type of computer over a desktop computer in education and rehabilitation is that it can be used during treatment sessions and then brought home for practice.

Many school systems have decided to use a laptop called the Google Chromebook (http://google.com/chromebook) due to its relatively low cost and many helpful included features that benefit students.

TABLET COMPUTERS

Tablet computers look like the screen of a laptop. They may run a different operating system than desktops or laptops.

Instead of a conventional keyboard, tablets often have a touch screen that is activated with a finger or special pen/stylus as well as an onscreen keyboard to navigate and add data directly onto the screen.

Peripheral devices such as external keyboards that use Bluetooth can be used.

They can be docked to a station in order to use a keyboard, CD/DVD drive, or other peripherals if desired.

The iPad and Galaxy Tablet are currently very popular tablet computers, and quite a few others have become available.

HYBRIDS

Netbooks emerged in 2007 as small, lightweight, and inexpensive laptop computers primarily to be used for general computing and accessing the Internet and using web-based applications. They were initially much smaller than laptops, did not have DVD drives, and had quite a bit less memory and speed. They typically had a hard time running the newest operating systems because they didn't have enough power. Over the past few years the specifications of netbooks have merged with those of cheaper laptops. There are now "super compact netbook computers" which offer users most features of a larger computer, but are easier to type on than using a smartphone.

SMARTPHONES

iPhones, Android, and Windows phones have become widely used for education and rehabilitation. There are many products coming on the market that fall in this category and offer many benefits such as the following:

- They can be used to help with organization, data entry, and task management.
- Due to their small size, they are great if used to augment communication or to help with memory.
  - Many apps are offered that can make life more productive and enjoyable for users who have intact vision and fine motor control.
  - Accessories and special features such as portable full-size keyboards and text readers are available to make them easier to use. Internet access and cloud storage is now commonplace

and allows the transfer of data without cables or external services.

Despite these benefits, small devices are currently not appropriate for all users. There are several drawbacks:

- Good fine motor control and vision are needed to access the device if no assistive technology is used.
- The devices can be easily misplaced.
- The small screen is difficult on the eyes when used for sustained viewing.

SELECTION DEVICES

Whenever possible, it is a good idea to use mainstream products. However, there are a variety of peripheral devices that can be used to help people who have difficulty accessing devices.

MOUSE

When using a computer, the standard mouse may be fine for most people with good hand control. However, many people with disabilities have impaired fine motor movements and find it difficult to see the movement of the cursor on the computer screen. Some people are unable to use their dominant hand due to weakness, paralysis, or coordination deficits. The use of the mouse may be confusing for people with significant cognitive deficits, who may do better with a touch screen. Most operating systems enable us to customize the use of a mouse and cursor size.

TRACKBALLS

Trackballs are often a good solution for individuals with coordination difficulties with their hand because the cursor can be controlled with a finger. The device stays in one place as the user moves the ball. The BIGtrack is the largest trackball available. This large ball requires less fine motor control than a standard trackball and it is ruggedly built.

TOUCH SCREENS

Touch screens are now included as a feature of many of the newer devices. They are activated by touching the screen with a fingertip or stylus. This type of direct selection is often more effective and intuitive with younger children or individuals with significant cognitive deficits. Touch screens are used on most tablets and can be attached or integrated onto computer monitors.

SWITCHES

Technology is available to assist people with little or no use of their hands. People who have reliable movement of at least one part of their body can control the cursor on the screen. Reliable mouth movement or eye gaze can control a computer. Special switches make use of at least one muscle over which the individual has voluntary control, such as the head, knee, or mouth. To make selections, users use switches activated by movement. People who have severe mobility impairments often can use scanning and Morse code for computer access. Vendors offering a wide variety of switches are Enablemart (http://www.enablemart.com) and RehabMart (http://www.rehabmart.com). Switches for the iPad are available from RJ Cooper & Associates (http://www.rjcooper.com).

KEYBOARDS

Keyguards and keyboard overlays are helpful accessories when needed. They can decrease the number of unwanted keystrokes due to someone with poor manual coordination hitting more than one key at a time, keep the mechanics of a keyboard safe from the effects of spills and drooling, and help those who struggle to identify the keys.

Expanded keyboards that have larger keys spaced farther apart can replace standard keyboards for people with limited fine motor control. Mini-keyboards provide access for those who have fine motor control but lack the range of motion to use a standard keyboard. There are also keyboard trays with adjustable arms that can be purchased for individualized positioning of the user.

Most operating systems include special features that can help with keyboard use. To access those features, study the accessibility options of your operating system. The keyboards of many new devices include an image of a microphone. When the microphone is selected, the user can often speak and have the device type what is said aloud. More information about speech to text follows.

SPEECH INPUT

Speech input provides another option for people with disabilities who have difficulty typing. This feature may be referred to as speech recognition or speech to text (STT). Through speech-recognition technology, the user controls the computer or enters text by speaking into a microphone. Now, many mobile devices are able to automatically translate that spoken speech into written text. In the past, this was a much more difficult process because most computer software offering speech recognition needed to be trained to recognize specific voices. This is still the case if individuals have speech which is difficult to understand. Many professionals and families believe that speech to text is the ideal solution for students with written expression deficits. In order to effectively use speech to text, users need to speak distinctly in an organized way so that the resulting text is transcribed properly. It isn't always accurate and corrections may need to be made. Using speech to create text can be very difficult for people who have communication and cognitive deficits. I have had the most success with SpeakQ by Quillsoft (http://www.goqsoftware.com) on a PC as well as the Dragon Dictation app or integrated speech to text features on the newer mobile devices.

ENVIRONMENTAL CONTROL

Speech input can also be used for environmental control with environmental control units (ECUs). Commands can be said aloud for turning lights on and off, adjusting room temperature, and operating appliances when coupled with an environmental control unit or program. For more information about this type of technology, check out AbilityHub (http://www.abilityhub.com/speech/speech-ecu.htm) and AbilityNet GATE (http://abilitynet.wetpaint.com/page/Environmental+Control).

HEADSETS AND MICROPHONES

Much of the software described in this guide is for recording and listening to speech. Mobile devices now use built-in microphones and speakers that are far superior to computers used in the past. If the technology is going to be used in a quiet environment and the use of sound won't disturb others, then additional purchases may not be needed. If you are working with these assistive tools where there are distractions and others need quiet, it is often a sound investment to purchase a good set of headphones with a built-in microphone and external noise reduction features for use with voice recording and speech recognition software.

If the user uses a hearing aid or is not comfortable with a headset, a desktop microphone can be purchased.

ADDITIONAL RESOURCES

There are many articles, blogs, YouTube videos, and websites that offer more information on products mentioned above. Below are some resources to help you learn more about the selection and purchase of hardware and peripherals for assistive technology.

- **AbilityHub:** http://www.abilityhub.com
- **Apple Accessibility:** http://www.apple.com/accessibility
- **AssistiveTech.net:** http://www.assistivetech.net
- **Dynavox Mayer-Johnson:** http://www.mayer-johnson.com
- **EnableMart:** http://www.enablemart.com
- **Microsoft Accessibility:** http://www.microsoft.com/enable
- **Pass it On Center:** http://www.passitoncenter.org (A center to foster the appropriate reuse of AT)
- **RehabTool.com:** http://www.rehabtool.com
- **RJ Cooper & Associates:** http://www.rjcooper.com

CHAPTER 4

TECHNOLOGY AND STRATEGIES TO
IMPROVE VERBAL EXPRESSION

In this chapter, assistive technologies are highlighted that can be used to enhance verbal expression. A multimedia approach using sound, text, and pictures helps with verbal communication. All children, especially those with special needs, learn best to verbally communicate when they repeatedly hear words, see images and objects, and associate utterances with meaning. Products that offer the ability to record speech are especially effective.

A GOOD DIAGNOSIS WITH PROFESSIONAL INPUT IS CRITICAL

Prior to the selection of products, it's essential to analyze the major obstacles of speaking and figure out what is needed to improve it. Verbal expression deficits can be the result of motor, structural, and pragmatic impairments from injuries or disorders such as:

- developmental delay,
- articulation disorder,
- language and learning disability,
- Down syndrome,
- cleft palate,
- autism spectrum disorder,
- foreign accent,

- learning English as a second language,
- hearing loss,
- voice disorder,
- dysarthria (slurred speech from low tone or weakness),
- head injury, or
- apraxia (motor-sequencing issue).

Even though many technology tools are very affordable and easy to obtain, they are most appropriate when used under the guidance or direction of a speech-language pathologist who specializes in speech development and production as well as expressive language skills. Finding a good app or other technology tool to match the needs of the user is part of the challenge, but knowing how to use the tools to actually improve skills is an even greater challenge. It may take a skilled therapist to accurately determine which sounds need help and to properly teach the correct way to produce specific sounds or groups of sounds or to determine which words to include on a communication device and determine how best to help the child learn to communicate.

STRATEGIES TO ENCOURAGE VERBAL EXPRESSION

In addition to obtaining a proper diagnosis, it is important to use conventional strategies for helping people who struggle to make themselves understood.

Here are some guidelines to consider while developing expressive communication skills:

- Be patient and provide additional response time.
- Encourage total communication—use speech with other avenues of expression unless formally working to improve one targeted skill during a formal treatment session.
- Provide consistent expectations for speaking across all environments.
- Set the stage for frequent opportunities for practicing new skills in structured and unstructured settings. Many repetitions are critical for learning.
- Offer visual supports to promote learning and enhance communication.
- Use engaging, meaningful, age-appropriate stimuli.
- Record the individual's verbal utterances to increase self-awareness and motivation.

INFORMATIVE ONLINE RESOURCES

There are a number of online resources that offer a wealth of information for families as well as professionals so that they become more aware of expected speech and language milestones and can benefit from descriptions of activities to promote verbal expression. Resources include organizations, social networking sites, speech pathology blogs, websites, Pinterest boards, and wikis. An example of each type of online resource is included below. Many more exist. If you don't see what you are looking for, try searching online. Many people don't take advantage of these tremendous resources which are available for free.

Organizations:

- **The American Speech-Language Hearing Association:** http://www.asha.org
- **Apraxia-KIDS:** http://www.apraxia-kids.org
- **The Stuttering Foundation:** http://www.stutteringhelp.org

Social Networking Sites:

- **Facebook Groups:** SLPs Talk Apps, IPad Apps and info for Special Kids, Speech and Language Therapy, Augmentative Communication Resources & Help
- **LinkedIn Groups:** American Speech-Language-Hearing Association, Assistive Technology Professionals, Early Intervention Professionals, International Society for Technology in Education, K12 Assistive Technology Professionals, Technology Integration in Education

Speech Pathology Blogs/Websites/Wikis:

- **Glenda Anderson:** http://atclassroom.blogspot.com
- **Lois Jean Brady:** http://proactivespeech.wordpress.com
- **Stephanie Bruno:** http://community.advanceweb.com/blogs/sp_1/default.aspx
- **Barbara Fernandes:** http://www.geekslp.com
- **Joan L. Green:** http://www.innovativespeech.com/blog
- **Becca Jarzynski:** http://www.talkingkids.org
- **Cindy Meester:** http://meesterc.wordpress.com
- **Eric Sailers:** http://speechlanguagepathologysharing.blogspot.com
- **Sean Sweeney:** http://www.speechtechie.com

MANY TECH TOOLS ARE AVAILABLE TO HELP

A large number of resources are available to help improve expressive communication skills such as articulation, word retrieval, sentence formulation, fluency, and dialogue. Some products are very structured, provide feedback, and are intuitive in terms of the increasing level of difficulty, while others require more skill to use. There are also dedicated communication devices, apps, and other assistive technologies that can be effectively used to augment communication.

MOBILE DEVICES AND APPS

There has been an explosion of apps and features in mobile technology devices that can be used to improve and augment verbal expression. Many are listed in this chapter. The majority of items listed can be used on iDevices such as an iPad or iPhone. Some can be used on phones and tablets using the Android, Windows, or other operating system. Many of the online sites mentioned can be accessed from any type of device unless they require built-in software to view, such as Flash, which may not be available on a device. This can get a bit complicated. Interactive Flash-based sites may be unable to be used from an iPad, but there are some Flash apps for iDevices that enable users to see some Flash content.

The websites for each described product are given to provide you with information that is more detailed regarding versions of the product, networking ability, compatible operating systems, and availability of online tutorials or demos. The prices written in this guide are generally for an individual full-featured home version of each item. These prices will undoubtedly change, but they are included to give a ballpark estimate.

Here are a few guidelines you may find helpful:

- Be sure to check the store that is used for your particular devices for operating system compatibility. For iDevices, go to the app store on your device or download software to your computer at http://www.itunes.com. For Android devices, there is a range of stores, depending on your device. It may be easiest to search from your device or visit http://www.android.com/apps. For Windows apps, visit http://windows.microsoft.com/en-us/windows-8/apps. You need to have Windows 8 to interact with the store.
- Confirm the most current description in the store to make sure the information on features and prices is up to date.
- Read reviews from users while in the store prior to purchase and to look at other apps people have purchased. Searching online for reviews can also help. Negative reviews should not necessarily deter

you from trying a product. I occasionally find that what others don't find helpful, I may consider a goldmine. In addition, it is often the very dissatisfied user who posts a negative review. There may be many more satisfied users who don't take the time to express themselves.

- Many apps or websites include video tutorials produced by the developer. There may also be instructional videos on YouTube that offer additional insights about how to use the app.
- Apps often have lite versions to try before purchasing the fully featured version.
- Lock the student in an app if needed. If you are using an iDevice running iOS 6.0 or later, you can take advantage of the Guided Access feature, which is password protected and prevents an individual from prematurely exiting an app.

BE CREATIVE

Please keep in mind that many of the apps listed can be used in creative ways to maximize their effectiveness. Try not to look at the app as a static product that you can only use in the way that it was developed to be used. For example:

- Passively viewing a flash card will not be as effective at stimulating language as it would be if a parent, teacher, or therapist turns the activity into a more interactive experiential activity.
- An individual who needs help with social skills may benefit from using apps in a group situation to improve turn taking or conversational skills.
- A speech recognition app can be used to practice speaking clearly.
- A text to speech app that reads text aloud can be used to practice saying multisyllabic words aloud.

IMPROVING VERBAL EXPRESSION SKILLS

When selecting the most appropriate technology to either improve or compensate for verbal expression skills, it is necessary to figure out which types of features will most help the individual.

- **Close-up video of mouth movement:** This is often very helpful for people with verbal apraxia, which is a motor coordination problem.
- **Multisensory stimuli:** Just about all learners do best when multiple senses are used. New learning is enhanced when the individual hears words, sees words and images, and can record his or her voice.

However, there are some individuals who find multisensory stimulation to be too much, and they do best with stimulating just one sense at a time.

- **Pictures and words shown in natural settings:** It is often helpful for people with language and cognitive deficits to see pictures of items in context or grouped by category.

- **Practice on specific speech sounds:** Apps that empower the user to quickly create practice items with very specific sounds and then use them repeatedly to practice listening to and saying words and phrases aloud are very effective. These programs are helpful for people who have motor speech issues such as apraxia and inarticulate speech, as well as for people who are working on improving clarity and fluency of connected speech.

- **Authoring and customizing capability:** Programs that include the ability to customize the stimuli items by adding pictures and recordings as well as removing images or text that are not helpful to practice are beneficial for learning to say personalized information and for creating practice materials that are relevant for each person.

- **Recording capability:** Many individuals with expressive deficits benefit from hearing recordings of their speech immediately after they speak. It is very helpful for people who are unable to decipher the accuracy of their response.

- **High-level language with cognitive challenges:** People with subtle verbal expression deficits may appear "normal" in basic conversation. They may be quite capable of performing straightforward language tasks such as repeating sentences and naming pictures. However, the performance of these individuals often deteriorates when reasoning and memory components are added to the task. Deficits are often exacerbated when the students are asked to describe solutions to problems, complete analogies, or summarize written material. As tasks become more abstract, the response becomes more difficult. There are many products listed in the chapter on cognitive therapy that may be helpful for these students.

- **Text readers:** Text-reading software reads text aloud from the computer or mobile device. The multisensory input can be very helpful when working to improve verbal expression. Word lists, phrases, and sentences can be read aloud using technology either before or after the individual says them aloud. Usually the rate of speech and voice can be changed.

- **Topic-based sentences, dialogue tasks/scripts, and programs encouraging verbal narrative:** Many individuals with verbal expression deficits need help establishing carryover with new artic-ulatory patterns, fluent speech, word retrieval strategies, and the organization of content in connected discourse. Technology can be used as a context for this type of practice in many ways. The parents, teacher, therapist, or a computer buddy can provide communication models and work toward verbal communication goals while using engaging activities.

- **Visual or graphic feedback of speech and voice production:** Some people are very motivated when they see something happen on the screen when they verbally produce something correctly.
- **Speech to text:** Software speech to text features will type what the user dictates. This in itself can be quite motivating for accurate ver-bal production. There is also some software that "grades" whether or not speech is produced correctly rather than just recording it for playback.
- **Data collection:** Some products keep track of the accuracy of a user's response (automatically or with input from the adult user) and are able to document progress.
- **Multiple users:** There are apps that enable multiple participants to take turns using the product with features customized for each person in a group.

IMPROVING SPEECH INTELLIGIBILITY

People who have dysarthria (slurred speech), a heavy foreign accent, verbal apraxia (speech-motor programming problems), developmental articulation errors, dysfluent speech (stuttering), speech that is too fast or monotone, or impaired speech due to hearing impairments can ben-efit from software products for improving speech patterns. It is critical to know if the individual's articulation challenges are developmental in nature, caused by a motor coordination issue (verbal apraxia), or caused by a musculature weakness (dysarthria). The resources listed in this section should be used in very different ways depending on the etiology of the deficit.

Features of these products may include:

- a focus on the production of particular sounds;
- the ability to select the position(s) of sounds in words;
- sounds in isolation, words, phrases, sentences, and stories;
- thousands of target words and pictures;
- the ability to select more than one sound and combine the images;

- a description of how to physically form sounds using text and diagrams;
- pictures and videos of up-close mouth movements;
- recordings of the sounds for users to listen to and repeat (may be helpful for people who can't perceive the accuracy of their response or a hindrance for people who find it distracting);
- a focus on the minimal pairs approach to develop discrimination and production of sounds (the words presented differ by a single sound, which changes the meaning);
- the ability to convert the speech to text;
- immediate feedback on the accuracy of the user's speech;
- computer-based visual biofeedback in graphic representations for pitch, volume, intonation pattern, easy onset of phonation, and articulatory precision;
- games and activities using selected sounds;
- the ability to use alone or with a group of students; and
- use of delayed auditory feedback to promote fluency.

MOBILE DEVICE APPS FOR IMPROVING ARTICULATION AND SPEECH INTELLIGIBILITY

Apraxia Picture Sound Cards
by Foundations Developmental House, LLC
http://www.fdhkids.com/apps_and_materials.html
- This app is geared for use by speech-language pathologists to sort cards by specific speech sounds movements and motor plans.
- The app includes video of Speech-EZ® hand cues, a goal bank, and a parent as well as a professional version.
- iOS
- $179.99

Apraxia Ville
by Smarty Ears
http://smartyearsapps.com/service/apraxia-ville
- Provides animated video modeling of consonants and vowels and words by syllable structure (e.g., CV, VC, CVC, and CVCV). Multisyllabic words are also provided.
- Content can be customized and data can be tracked.
- iOS
- $29.99

Articulate it!

by Smarty Ears

http://smartyearsapps.com/service/articulate-it

- Contains more than 1,000 images to help children improve speech sound production in words and phrases in flash card and matching game modes.
- Offers ability to customize words and images, record student utterances, save data, and generate homework.
- iOS
- $38.99

Articulation Flip Books

by Dynavox Mayer Johnson

http://www.mayer-johnson.com/category/apps/say-it-right-flip-books-app

- Students "read aloud" silly sentence stories comprised of three individual panels by swiping the screen to combine fragments.
- Each word or phrase can be said aloud to provide a speech model.
- iOS
- The free version of this app includes the /r/ sound. Additional sounds cost about $9.99.

Articulation Games

by Virtual Speech Center

http://www.virtualspeechcenter.com/Resources/articulation_games_app.aspx

- This app includes thousands of flash cards with audio of more than 48 sounds used in four different customizable games.
- The free version of this app includes the /b/ sound.
- Android and iOS
- $19.99

Articulation Scenes

by Smarty Ears

http://smartyearsapps.com/service/articulation-scenes

- Provides engaging games that allow children to practice sounds in fun activities with a cinema theme.
- Includes 72 scenes with four different activities and more than 1,200 practiced words.
- Offers prerecorded audio, ability to record voice, data tracking, and homework sheets.
- iOS
- $34.99

Articulation Station

by Little Bee Speech

http://www.littlebeespeech.com/articulation_station.php

- There are six engaging practice activities at the word, sentence, and story level for each sound.
- Audio recordings and data can be saved.
- Free for /p/ sound and individual sounds can be purchased for a few dollars.
- iOS
- $49.99 for Pro version.

ArtikPix- Full

by Expressive Solutions LLC

http://www.expressive-solutions.com.artikpix.html

- A fully featured app including 24 decks for sounds with a total of more than 1,000 cards.
- Unique features include video recording capability and ability to combine decks.
- Users can add customized cards, work in groups and keep data for each user, and see themselves while producing the words.
- iOS
- $29.99 for complete version.
- Free for just the "th, w, y and h" deck.

Dragon Apps

by Nuance

http://www.nuancemobilelife.com/apps

- There are a number of different Dragon apps, such as Dragon Dictation for iOS and Dragon Mobile Assistant for Android, that use voice recognition technology to convert spoken words into text. It's very motivating for students who are working to improve speech intelligibility to speak clearly and try to have the device type what they say.
- There are now quite a few voice recognition features included right in the keyboard of many devices, but this app is helpful especially for older devices, such as the second generation iPad.
- It requires the Internet to work.
- Android, Blackberry, and iOS
- Free

Drillaby Pro

by SLP Tech Tools

http://www.slptechtools.com

- This is for young children to provide articulation practice with an engaging game.
- Sounds groups can be produced using accents from the U.S., U.K., or Australia.
- iOS
- $24.99 for full version.
- Free for one sound pair.

First Phrases

by Hamaguchi Apps

http://www.hamaguchiapps.com/

- This engaging animated app records users producing two or three word phrases.
- The child will hear him- or herself speak the phrase and see an animated character follow his or her direction that was said, such as "Pour the milk."
- Great for carry-over of learned speech sounds.
- This app takes up a lot of memory and requires more than the typical amount of time to load.
- There is also a lite version.
- iOS
- $15.99

I Can Articulate

by Express SLP

http://www.expressslp.com

- This app is helpful for working with students of all ages at word, sentence, and story level.
- There are approximately 2,500 photo images spread across 46 sounds.
- The SLP version of this app is very helpful when transcribing a recorded speech sample and selecting target sounds and positions to work on in therapy. Results of the session can be shown in a graph for visual comparison of accuracy.
- iOS
- $39.99 for full version.
- Free version with the /k/ sound; additional sounds can be purchased for a few dollars.

Minimal Pairs Academy

by Smarty Ears

http://smartyearsapps.com/service/minimal-pairs-academy

- There is an engaging minimal pairs introduction, then activities involving listening and speaking at the word and phrase level.
- Data tracking is available.
- iOS
- $39.99

Multiple Choice Articulation

by Erik S. Raj

http://www.erikxraj.com

- This app includes hundreds of sound-specific multiple choice questions to work on saying sounds in sentences.
- There are amusing and thought-provoking audio questions and answers that are ideal for working on carryover of sounds into sentences and conversation.
- It includes the most commonly mispronounced sounds, such as /s/, /z/, /r/, /l/ blends and SH, CH, and TH.
- iOS
- $4.99

Phonics Studio

by GrasshopperApps.com

http://itunes.apple.com/us/app/phonics-studio/id547795266?mt=8

- This app includes more than 2,500 flash cards that are divided into sound groups. Users can record themselves speaking and save the utterances as well as add pictures and categories.
- iOS
- Free

PhonoPix- Full

by Expressive Solutions LLC

http://www.expressive-solutions.com/phonopix.html

- This app includes activities using minimal pairs to contrast incorrect and correct speech sound production.
- There are 10 decks with 40 minimal pairs in each.
- Features include flash card and matching activities, listening to and recording audio, and collecting scores for multiple students.
- iOS
- $29.99

Pocket Artic

by Synapse Apps

http://pocketslp.com/our-apps/pocket-artic

- This app provides more than 3,000 stimulus cards for 29 sounds at the word, phrase, or sentence level in the initial, medial, or final position.
- Detailed scoring features and results.
- Android and iOS
- $9.99

Pocket Pairs

by Synapse Apps

http://pocketslp.com/our-apps/pocket-pairs

- This is a minimal pairs app that targets the 12 most common phonological processes, such as cluster reduction and fronting of speech sounds.
- It offers a receptive as well as expressive mode, images that highlight correct and incorrect articulatory placement, and data tracking.
- Android and iOS
- $6.99

R Intensive SLP

by Smarty Ears

http://smartyearsapps.com/service/intensive

- This app includes three games for practicing the R at the word, phrase, and sentence levels.
- The /r/ sound is divided into nine subgroups, depending on the position in the word and surrounding sounds.
- iOS
- $19.99

Speech Box for Speech Therapy

by The Jonah Bonah Learning Company

http://www.speechboxapp.com

- Tap on a box and it displays its pictures organized by content. Tap on a picture and it is enlarged and said aloud if desired.
- Seven hundred pictures are included, grouped by sounds and categories.
- It is easy to add more pictures, boxes, notes, and customize tasks.
- iOS
- $19.99

Speech Cards Professional

by RWH Technology

http://www.rwhtechnology.com/apps/speech-cards

- This app allows users to create flash cards with pictures, text, and sound.
- Configure the flash card the way that is best to use with an individual to practice their speech, then use the microphone to practice speaking and listen for the immediate feedback.
- Cards can be shared with others.
- iOS
- $9.99

Speech Flipbook

by Tactus Therapy Solutions

http://tactustherapy.com/apps/speechflipbook

- This app can be used to work on many aspects of verbal expression, such as articulation and phonological awareness.
- It is set up like a traditional flipbook, and you choose what the student needs to work on.
- This app is easy to set up and allows flexibility when choosing between sounds and words.
- iOS
- $6.99

Speech Pairs

by Synapse Apps, LLC

http://pocketslp.com/our-apps/speech-pairs

- This is a home version of the "Minimal Pairs" app, created for parents and home practice.
- The two words presented differ by only one sound. Students can listen to the words repeatedly and record themselves as well as view diagrams.
- There are "say" and "listen" practice activities.
- The app includes tips on how to improve sounds, milestones, and diagrams.
- Android and iOS
- $2.99

Speech Sounds on Cue for iPad
by Multimedia Speech Pathology
http://www.mmsp.com.au/speech-sounds-on-cue-for-ipad
- This is ideal for students who have significant speech impairments who benefit from watching up-close lip movement, phrase completions, and the inclusion of both pictures and text.
- More than 500 video clips are included.
- Recording, playback, and rhyming words are included.
- iOS
- $22.99
- Free trial version comes with one sound.

Speech Stickers
by Serious Tree LLC
http://www.serioustree.com/products/speechstickers/index.html
- This is one of my favorite apps to use with young children who need to be motivated to practice early consonant and vowel sounds. The adult customizes the app to work on the targeted sounds and the child is rewarded for speech repetitions.
- iOS
- $14.99

Speech Therapy for Apraxia- NACD
by Blue Whale
http://www.nacd.org/speech_sound/apps.php
- Various levels encourage production of single syllables from eight different consonant groups.
- The app uses pictures and audio for each level.
- It works on motor programming for speech.
- Android and iOS
- $4.99

Speech With Milo Articulation Board Game
by Doonan Speech Therapy
http://www.speechwithmilo.com/apps
- This is a very interactive and engaging board game. Students practice target sounds in initial, medial, and final positions.
- Data can be tracked.
- iOS
- $6 for a few sounds
- $24.99 for Pro version with all sounds.

VAST Autism 1- Core
by Speak in Motion
http://www.speakinmotion.com/solutions/mobile-apps/vast-autism-1-core
- This app was designed to help children with autism and motor speech challenges such as apraxia.
- It combines an up-close video of speaker's mouth with written words and auditory cues to model sounds, words, phrases, and sentences which are concrete and can be practiced during the day.
- A mirror feature promotes oral motor sequencing and self-monitoring.
- iOS
- $4.99

MOBILE DEVICE APPS FOR INITIATION OF PHONATION (SOUND PRODUCTION), VOICE, FLUENCY, RATE AND RHYTHM

Bla Bla Bla
by Lorenzo Bravi
http://www.lorenzobravi.com/projects/bla-bla-bla
- This app encourages voicing. Amusing visual feedback is shown when children use their voice.
- iOS
- Free

Conversation Paceboard
by Lorraine Curran
https://www.facebook.com/AptusSLT
- This app is designed to work on slowing down the rate of speech to improve intelligibility.
- There are six circles to use for pacing and hundreds of questions to use to stimulate practice with speech.
- A variety of graphics and feedback assist with monitoring speech rate.
- iOS
- $3.99

DAF Assistant
by ARTEFACT, LLC
http://artefactsoft.com/index.htm
- This app uses Delayed Auditory Feedback (DAF) and Frequency-shifting Auditory Feedback (FAF) techniques that are known to provide a "chorus" effect to help people with stuttering to speak more fluently.
- Android and iOS
- $4.99 Android and $9.99 iOS

SlowTunes
by Brian Stokes
http://slowtunesapp.com
- This app slows down the rate of all voice output without changing the pitch.
- iOS
- $1.99

Sonneta Voice Monitor
by MintLeaf Software Inc.
http://mintleafsoftware.com/voice-monitor.html
- This app provides a real-time visual display to measure vocal pitch and sound level.
- iOS
- $49.99

Speech Cards Professional
by RWH Technology
http://www.rwhtechnology.com/apps/speech-cards
- This app lets users create flash cards with pictures, text, and sound.
- Configure the flash card the way that is best to use with an individual to practice his or her speech, then use the microphone to practice speaking and listen for the immediate feedback.
- The cards can be shared with others.
- iOS
- $9.99

Speech Prompts
by Handhold Adaptive
http://www.handholdadaptive.com/SpeechPrompts.html
- This app includes a series of exercises to work on rate, rhythm, intonation, and loudness.
- Real-time feedback is presented visually in wave forms and graphics.
- Sensitivity can be changed to accommodate sounds in the environment and goals of the student.
- iOS
- $19.99

In addition to using apps that feature drill-and-practice techniques to improve speech sound production mentioned above, the use of text readers that will read words aloud that are highlighted and speech recognition software that will type what you say can be very helpful. Word and sentence lists can be written into documents that the computer reads aloud. Users can practice reading aloud and then listen to the computer for help as needed or to check their responses.

TECHNOLOGY TO IMPROVE EXPRESSIVE LANGUAGE

There are many students who are able to articulate sounds well but who have "language" deficits. These deficits may be severe, as in the case of nonverbal individuals with autism spectrum disorder, or very mild, as in the case when a person has difficulty thinking of specific words. There is also a social component to the use of language.

Software and apps that are helpful for improving expressive language may focus on the following skills:
- augmentative and alternative communication (AAC; please refer to Chapter 5);
- word retrieval/naming;
- phrase and sentence formulation;
- functional scripts; and
- dialogue/conversation.

People who have word-retrieval problems, delayed language, an expressive language disorder, or who are learning English as a second language need to improve their ability to think of words before they are able to say them. They also need to practice using words in phrases and sentences to convey meaning. Some of the practice items use text only, some use pictures alone or pictures with text, and others have authoring capability so that the user can use personalized information to practice.

IMPROVING WORD KNOWLEDGE AND RETRIEVAL

Word-finding difficulties can result in significant expressive language problems. Most of us have encountered the experience of knowing a word but being unable to think of it. In structured therapy sessions this may take place when being asked to name an image, formulate a sentence, explain an answer, or list items in a category. The best way to practice retrieving words is to actually practice retrieving the words during a wide variety of activities. Often, in school, the emphasis is on learning new meanings of words. In many instances, students may have learned definitions but be unable to show what they know because of word retrieval deficits. When teaching word knowledge, it is helpful to talk about meanings, synonyms, and describing skills.

Websites with helpful information and suggestions for enhancing word retrieval include:

- **Diane German, Ph.D.:** http://www.wordfinding.com. Dr. German is an expert in the area of word retrieval diagnosis and treatment and produced this website, which includes information about diagnosis, treatment, and IEP goals for children with word finding deficits.
- **Caroline Bowen, Ph.D.:** http://speech-language-therapy.com. Click on "Articles" and you will see a large amount of very helpful information regarding diagnosis and intervention. Included on this site is information about what word retrieval difficulties are and what can be done to help.

Websites to enhance word knowledge and retrieval include:

- **Rhymezone:** http://www.rhymezone.com. This website helps find rhymes, synonyms, definitions, related words, and more.
- **Vocabulary.co.il:** http://www.vocabulary.co.il. This website includes many games for improving word retrieval.

APPS TO IMPROVE WORD KNOWLEDGE AND WORD RETRIEVAL

ABA Flashcards- Actions

by Kindergarten.com

http://www.kindergarten.com (This website provides many helpful suggestions regarding how to use the apps they produce.)

- This is one in a series of apps that provide interactive flash cards.
- New features include the ability to select specfic pictures, text, audio and or track data during practice.
- iOS
- Most of the apps cost $1.99.

Describe It

by Synapse Apps, LLC

http://pocketslp.com/our-apps/describe-slp

- Provides audio cues for describing, such as taste, touch, function, sight, hearing, smell, and category.
- There is a "study" section and two games to play: "Pass It" in which the user describes items to teammates and "Guess It" in which the user touches clues and tries to guess a word.
- iOS
- $6.99

Describe It to Me

by Smarty Ears

http://smartyearsapps.com/service/describe

- This app uses a game format to enhance deeper understanding of the semantic relationships between words.
- It can be used with groups, is customizable, and provides home-work sheets.
- iOS
- $9.99

Heads Up

by Warner Bros.

http://www.ellentv.com/page/2013/04/23/heads-up

- This is a game in which players give clues to each other to try to guess the word they are holding above their head.
- Android and iOS
- $.99

Learn to Talk First Words- Preschool, Kindergarten Flash Cards
by Thunderloop
http://www.thunderloop.com/first-words
- This app uses colorful flash cards with developmentally ordered content and voice output to teach words.
- iOS
- $1.99

Let's Name . . . Things Fun Deck
by Super Duper Publications
http://www.superduperinc.com/apps/apple.aspx#freeApple
- This app provides 53 pictured cards with written prompts that can be read aloud, such as "Let's name things you'd take on a trip."
- Android and iOS
- Free

Multiple Meanings Library
by Virtual Speech Center
https://www.virtualspeechcenter.com/Resources/multiple_meanings_app.aspx
- When using this app, students are presented with five different ways to learn multiple meanings of words: auditory bombardment, picture identification, definition, fill in, and make up sentences.
- iOS
- $12.99

My Pictures Talk
by Grembe Inc.
http://www.grembe.com/mpt
- Use this app to add text and audio to pictures and upload videos to use to practice verbal expression skills.
- iOS
- $4.99

Naming TherAppy
by Tactus Therapy Solutions Ltd.
http://www.tactustherapy.com/apps/naming
- This app is ideal for students who are older or don't do well with animations and younger-looking apps. Initially created to help adults with aphasia (a language impairment most often resulting

from a stroke), this app offers four sections: naming practice, naming test, describe, and flash cards.

- This app offers many customizable options for naming and description skills and you can add your own images to practice.
- This app is also available as part of Tactus Therapy's Language TherAppy app.
- iOS
- $24.99
- There is also a free version to try.

Word Retrieval
by Virtual Speech Center
http://www.virtualspeechcenter.com

- This app offers a wide variety of activities to practice, such as confrontation naming, associations, naming items in categories (divergent naming), and naming items from cues (convergent naming).
- iOS
- $9.99

STRATEGIES AND TECHNOLOGIES THAT CAN BE USED ON MOBILE DEVICES TO IMPROVE SPEAKING IN PHRASES AND SENTENCES

There are many ways to work on expanding words to phrases and phrases to sentences. Quite a lot is known about language development and the proper progression. Websites have been provided for reference. Many students find it motivating and engaging when their verbalizations are recorded and played back. These apps lend themselves to working on a wide variety of verbal expression goals. It's also very effective to begin early in the process by empowering students learning to speak by creating engaging activities encouraging verbal expression so that they can direct the behavior of others with words and expand their ability to request and make things happen.

In addition to the products discussed in this chapter, there are many products that are included in chapters talking about improving auditory comprehension, reading, and writing that can creatively be used to improve verbal expression. Below I have highlighted those that I find myself using the most often to improve a student's ability to speak in phrases and sentences.

Autism Language Learning
by TalkTime Pediatric Speech Academy

http://autismlanguagelearning.net

- This app uses functional real-life video rather than pictures to teach action words. It includes 54 targeted actions and about 80 video clips to work on expressive skills such as using pronouns and present tense. Past tense can be targeted after the clip stops. Rhythmic voice output and text can be turned on or off.
- iOS
- $19.99

First Phrases
by Hamaguchi Apps

http://www.hamaguchiapps.com/First_Phrases_App.html

- This is a great app for learning how to put two and three words together. Amusing characters are shown responding to directives by the user, at first by word selection, then by hearing the student's recording and following the directions such as "Turn on the water."
- iOS
- $15.99
- Free trial version

Language Builder
by Mobile Education Store LLC

http://mobile-educationstore.com/apps/narrative-skills/language-builder-for-ipad-2

- This app presents real-life pictures of children engaged in activities and tasks the user to record themselves saying sentences. Hints are available.
- iOS
- $9.99

Language Lab: Core Words
by Prentke Romich Company

https://aaclanguagelab.com/applab/core-words

- This is one in a series of developmentally appropriate apps to build expressive speaking skills to direct activities, make requests, and label items.
- iOS
- Free

Sentence Maker
by GrasshopperApps.com
http://www.itunes.apple.com/us/app/sentence-maker/id499150658?mt=8
- This app includes sentences grouped into 30 categories (total number of words or carrier phrases) to facilitate customization. Visual and auditory cues can be turned on or off.
- iOS
- $.99

Speech With Milo Verbs
by Doonan Speech Therapy
http://www.speechwithmilo.com
- This is one in a series of great Milo apps that is very engaging for encouraging children to speak in phrases and sentences. Milo the mouse performs more than 100 actions using animation. It is customizable.
- iOS
- $2.99

Tense Builder
by Mobile Education Store
http://mobile-educationstore.com/apps/parts-of-speech/tense-builder
- This app includes approximately 50 verbs with movies showing past, present, and future using humor to engage students. Several activities are available to improving receptive and expressive skills. Users can record sentences.
- iOS
- $19.99

APPS FOR TEACHING ACTIONS AND DIRECTING OTHERS

Autism Language Learning
by TalkTime Pediatric Speech Academy
http://autismlanguagelearning.net
- iOS
- $19.99

First Phrases
by Hamaguchi Apps
http://www.hamaguchiapps.com/First_Phrases_App.html
- iOS
- $15.99

Language Lab: Core Words
by Prentke Romich Company
https://aaclanguagelab.com/applab/core-words
- iOS
- Free

Language Lab: Directing Activities
by Prentke Romich Company
https://aaclanguagelab.com/applab/directing-activities
- iOS
- $1.99

APPS FOR VERB AGREEMENT AND TENSE

iPractice Verbs
by Smarty Ears
http://www.smartyears.com/service/ipractice-verbs
- iOS
- $4.99

Is & Are Fun Deck
by Super Duper Publications
http://www.superduperinc.com/apps
- Android and iOS
- $2.99

Language Lab: ing Verbs + Prepositions
by Doonan Speech Therapy
https://aaclanguagelab.com/applab/ing-verbs-and-prepositions
- iOS
- $2.99

Tense Builder
by Mobile Education Store
http://mobile-educationstore.com/apps/parts-of-speech/tense-builder
- iOS
- $19.99

APPS FOR TEACHING PRONOUNS

Autism Language Learning
by TalkTime Pediatric Speech Academy
http://autismlanguagelearning.net
- iOS
- $19.99

Pronoun Fill-in Super Fun Dec
by Super Duper Publications
http://www.superduperinc.com/apps
- iOS
- $4.99

Using I and Me Fun Deck
by Super Duper Publications
http://www.superduperinc.com/apps
- Android and iOS
- $1.99

APPS FOR TEACHING PLURALS

Expedition with Plurals
by Virtual Speech Center Inc.
http://www.virtualspeechcenter.com/Resources/expeditionwithplurals_
app.aspx
- iOS
- $1.99

Language Lab: Plurals
by Prentke Romich Company
https://aaclanguagelab.com/applab/plurals
- iOS
- $15.99

Plurality
by Zorten Software, LLC
http://zorten.com/plurality
- iOS
- $1.99

Plurals Fun Deck
by Super Duper Publications
http://www.superduperinc.com/apps
- $1.99 Android, $2.99 iOS

APPS FOR TEACHING PREPOSITIONS

Preposition Builder
by Mobile Education Store
http://mobile-educationstore.com/apps/parts-of-speech/preposition-builder
- iOS
- $7.99

Preposition Remix
by Smarty Ears
http://www.smartyears.com/service/preposition-remix
- iOS
- $9.99

Speech with Milo: Prepositions
by Doonan Speech Therapy
http://www.speechwithmilo.com
- iOS
- $2.99

APPS FOR PRACTICE ASKING AND ANSWERING QUESTIONS:

"WH" Question Cards-Pro; Who, What, When, Where, and Why
by Super Duper Publications
http://www.superduperinc.com/apps
- iOS
- $11.99

WhQuestions
by Smarty Ears
http://www.smartyearsapps.com/service/whquestions
- iOS
- $9.99

Question Sleuth
by Zorten Software
http://zorten.com/plurality/question-sleuth
- iOS
- $1.99

Questions2Learn
by Speech Pups LLC
http://www.speechpups.com
- iOS
- $9.99

QuestionIt
by Language Learning Apps LLC
http://languagelearningapps.com/?page_id=4
- iOS
- $24.99

Question Builder
by Mobile Education Store
http://mobile-educationstore.com/apps/narrative-skills/question-builder
- iOS
- $5.99

What's in the bag?
by All4mychild
http://all4mychild.com
- iOS
- $.99

APPS USING VIDEO AND CUSTOMIZABLE PHOTOS

Autism Language Learning
by TalkTime Pediatric Speech Academy
http://autismlanguagelearning.net
- iOS
- $19.99

I Like Stories
by Grasshopper Apps
http://www.grasshopperapps.com/i-like-stories
- Many books are included that can be customized. Students can add their voice and text to each page.
- iOS
- $.99

Tapikeo
by Jean-Eudes Lepelletier
http://www.tapikeo.com
- Add pictures to a flexible grid design with captions and the ability to record audio.
- iOS
- $1.99 with in-app purchases.

WordToob: Language Learning with Video Modeling
by John Halloran
http://wordtoob.com
- iOS
- $9.99

STRATEGIES AND TECHNOLOGIES THAT CAN BE USED ON MOBILE DEVICES TO IMPROVE DIALOGUE AND ENGAGING IN CONVERSATION

There are many children who, on the surface, appear to be able to speak well and name pictures without difficulty, but when the task becomes more challenging, they struggle to be able to express themselves. These individuals may have difficulty communicating more complex desires, retrieving words, and formulating sentences or abstract thoughts. When working with people whose challenges are more subtle, it is helpful to focus on challenging tasks such as:

- recalling less common words or those with a cognitive component such as opposites or analogies;
- formulating novel sentences to describe complex pictures, steps in a task, or solutions to problems;
- giving verbal directions to someone and having him or her do what you say using an interactive experiential app; and
- engaging in dialogue for conversation-level practice.

Please be sure to read Chapter 12: Interactive Programs to Improve Cognition, Learning, and Memory. Many of the apps described can also be used to work on higher level expressive language skills.

- -

Absurd

by LOGO-Start Publishers

http://www.logo-art.eu/apps

- This app offers four levels of amusing black and white pictures with something wrong. There are 96 images. There is no voice output or recording capability. The individual is challenged to explain what is wrong in the picture.
- iOS
- $5.99

Clicky Sticky

by Merge Mobile Inc.

http://www.mergemobile.com/apps/clickysticky

- This app facilitates creative play by encouraging the user to tap on a sticker and then drag to a scene.
- Android and iOS
- $1.99

Conversation TherAppy

by Tactus Therapy Solutions Ltd.

http://tactustherapy.com/apps/conversation

- This app works on higher level expressive language, pragmatic, and cognitive communication goals for older children. There are more than 300 photos and 10 questions, each to stimulate discussion.
- iOS
- $24.99

Conversation Cards

by Wee Black Sheep Entertainment

http://weeblacksheep.com/apps/conversation-cards

- This app offers more than 100 random open-ended questions to spark conversation.
- iOS
- $1.99

Cookie Doodle

by Shoe the Goose

http://www.shoethegoose.com/CookieDoodle.aspx

- This is a very engaging app that centers around the activity of preparing, decorating, and eating a homemade cookie. There are many apps in this series.
- iOS and Windows
- $.99

ConversationBuilderTeen

by Mobile-Education Store

http://mobile-educationstore.com/apps/conversationbuilderteen

- This app helps teenagers learn to have multiexchange conversations with their peers in a variety of social settings. ConversationBuilder is designed to help elementary aged children.
- iOS
- $29.99

Functional Conversation

by Linguisystems

http://www.linguisystems.com/products/product/display?itemid=10850

- This app was created to use with older students to practice prompted conversations. It includes hundreds of topics and prompts.
- iOS
- $24.99

My Playhome

by Shimon Young

http://www.myplayhomeapp.com

- This app includes a virtual dollhouse with multiple rooms, characters, and items that can be manipulated with engaging effects. It's a wonderful app to use to practice giving verbal directions or doing something and then describing what you did.
- Android and iOS
- $3.99

StoryBuilder for iPad

by Mobile-Education Store

http://mobile-educationstore.com

- This app presents the user with a picture, then records answers to a series of questions about the picture. At the end, the connected

speech of the user can be played back without the intervening questions. This app can be used for many goals, including sentence formulation.
- iOS
- $7.99

Talking Train
by all4mychild
http://www.all4mychild.com
- This app provides visual support for simple storytelling, retelling about activities, and asking questions. Engines expand when tapped so users can add drawings or photos or text. Readers can record their speech and final stories can be e-mailed.
- iOS
- $4.99

Toca Hair Salon 2
by Toca Boca AB
http://tocaboca.com/game/toca-hair-salon-2
- In this app, the child runs a hair salon using many different hair styling tools and engaging effects and accessories. This is just one in a series of amazing apps.
- Android and iOS
- $3.99

Verbal Reasoning
by Virtual Speech Center Inc.
http://www.virtualspeechcenter.com/Resources/verbal_reasoning_app.aspx
- This app is meant to be used with children 12 years and up to work on critical thinking skills and reasoning. It includes activities such as determining probable causes and solutions situations, stating pros and cons to issues, and answering questions.
- iOS
- $12.99

You're the Storyteller
by Hamaguchi Apps
http://www.hamaguchiapps.com
- Children create a story and can record their voice for each page. The images are very engaging and students determine the story line.

- iOS
- $5.99

HELPFUL ONLINE PROGRAMS FOR IMPROVING VERBAL EXPRESSION

A review of these programs is beyond the scope of this guide, but they are made available for your reference. Most are geared toward helping second language learners.

- **Duolingo:** http://www.duolingo.com
- **Pangaea Learning:** http://www.pangaealearning.com
- **BBC Languages:** http://www.bbc.co.uk/languages
- **Live Mocha:** http://www.livemocha.com
- **LearnEnglish Kids:** http://www.learnenglishkids.britishcouncil.org
- **Byki (Before you know it):** http://www.byki.com
- **Rocket Languages:** http://www.rocketlanguages.com
- **Rosetta Stone:** www.rosettastone.com

CHAPTER 5

AUGMENTATIVE AND ALTERNATIVE COMMUNICATION

DEVICES, APPS, AND MORE

WHAT AUGMENTATIVE AND ALTERNATIVE COMMUNICATION IS AND HOW IT HELPS

There are many tools and resources that can be used to help improve as well as compensate for impaired verbal expression. Anyone who is having difficulty expressing themselves through spoken language alone has the potential to benefit from Augmentative and Alternative Communication (AAC). AAC focuses on helping individuals whose speech does not meet their communication needs. Consistency with treatment and training on the use of these tools is the key to the successful integration of them into a person's daily life. Family and close friends as well as teachers and colleagues need to be part of this process and learn how best to facilitate functional conversations with these assistive therapy tools.

If a student is unable to speak effectively, there are many assistive technologies that can be used to help. Voice output devices are also referred to in the literature as augmentive and alternative communication, augcom, and voice output communication aids (VOCA). The use of AAC to facilitate and augment speaking is not a crutch that will keep people from trying to speak. On the contrary, it can be used as a great tool to expand communication attempts and promote talking. AAC supports can be anything other than a person's speech that is used to communicate. There are many low-tech, mid-tech, and high-tech solutions that are produced to augment speech. There are also many apps that were not created to help with verbal expression, but can be used effectively to support communication.

Research has shown that the use of AAC can:

- have a very positive effect on speech production,
- promote social engagement, and
- reduce frustration.

INDIVIDUALS HELPED BY AAC

The field of AAC has approximately a 40-year history. For a long time, AAC was a field for individuals with complex communication needs, most often used when people could not speak at all and had significant motor issues such as cerebral palsy or degenerative neurological conditions such as Amyotrophic lateral sclerosis (ALS/ Lou Gehrig's Disease) or Multiple sclerosis (MS).

AAC is now often being used to help students with:

- autism spectrum disorders,
- apraxia of speech,
- delayed speech and language,
- intellectual disabilities,
- genetic disorders such as Down syndrome,
- vocal surgery,
- intubation, and
- limited English proficiency.

CURRENT AAC TRENDS

It used to be that if high-tech devices were desired, there was a formal process "controlled" by speech-language pathologists and other members of a team who would complete an evaluation and make recommendations. It took many months to complete the process, write reports, and wait for insurance coverage and delivery of the item. The individual then received expert help from professionals. Programming devices was cumbersome and although many devices truly changed the lives of many for the good, many others were abandoned. We are now in the midst of a huge change in the field of AAC. Potential AAC solutions are now less expensive, readily available to interested consumers, and being used to help a much wider variety of individuals. There have been rapid changes to the products available (especially on mobile devices), the service delivery model, and funding. There are now hundreds of AAC apps on mobile devices. They vary significantly in features, background research, customizability, and implementation support. There are positive and negative aspects to this development.

Positive: More people are able to benefit from the products. Individuals who have difficulty expressing themselves now have easier access to potential solutions to improve the quality of their lives. Affordable technologies are finding their way into the lives of individuals who in the past might have spent their lives unable to effectively communicate or with very long waits to obtain devices. Society is beginning to use AAC apps and devices to teach verbal language, not just to provide a means of communication for people with very severe physical deficits.

Negative: Many of the products that have been around for a long time have had years of research to support the many features they offer in terms of teaching language and facilitating verbal expression. New apps don't.

Helping individuals with significant communication impairments is a more complex task than one may initially realize. Many parents and inexperienced professionals who have less expertise in this field are taking the lead with AAC decisions. Often, less guidance is provided for successful implementation of the AAC. Very often, a comprehensive communication evaluation by an expert in the field is skipped, and a device is given to a student without a formal evaluation and trial period to assess the situation and implement procedures to promote success. Students, families, and teachers often experience frustration and the device is shelved.

Individuals who have complex communication needs (CCN) are frequently not provided with the most appropriate tools and training to develop and maximize their communication skills. There is no centralized quality control.

FIRST STEPS

Before actually using AAC, it is necessary to analyze the individual's:
- strengths, communication needs, goals, and interests;
- effect of cognitive, motor, and/or sensory impairments on their ability to learn and use nonverbal communication methods;
- sources of motivation and engagement;
- initiative in attempting to communicate;
- frequency, range of intent, and effectiveness of messages being communicated nonverbally; and
- communication partner's resourcefulness to stimulate communication and understand what's expressed.

I strongly encourage individuals to seek professional guidance from a qualified, experienced speech-language pathologist when choosing and using AAC devices and apps. When I work with individuals who have limited communication abilities, I have found that I often have to work with other apps to get the student ready to benefit from AAC. We may work at first on establishing joint attention, promoting the concept of cause and effect, and motivating individuals to initiate communication and interact with the device. I have found the built-in features of mobile devices with touch screens as well as the many free and low-cost apps make therapy very engaging and efficient in reaching these initial goals as well as helping people advance to more involved communication tasks.

Tablets with AAC apps are not necessarily the best solutions for individuals who have difficulty using their hands to touch pictures and words to be said aloud by a device. Not all consumer products—even those with many accessibility options such as the iPad—meet the needs of every person.

When working with individuals with severe autism spectrum disorder, the task of learning to use AAC apps to communicate is complex. It is a bit less complex when the lack of communication is due to speech or voice disorder as opposed to a language or cognitive disorder.

There are also individuals with significant physical disabilities who may need to use eye gaze or scanning to access the technology. A multidisciplinary team including a physical therapist, occupational therapist, speech-language pathologist, and an assistive technology expert is ideal in this situation. It is important that if a device is to be used with a person with significant physical limitations, the person selecting the tool and training the individual be familiar with issues relating to seating, positioning, and the apps that are switch-accessible as well as recent products using alternate ways to access the device.

An increasing number of products is becoming available for tablets, but the products are new. The research on their efficacy has just begun. Several apps or devices should be tried and data recorded and analyzed for effectiveness. If a tablet computer is indeed the product of choice, there is a great deal of planning that needs to go into configuring the device and teaching the individual how to most effectively use it. It is important to address the many communication functions when working on AAC—not just labeling pictures, as many inexperienced users have a tendency to do. Students have many reasons to communicate, such as to:

- engage in interactions with others and experience social closeness;
- participate in learning, school, and work;
- fulfill desires, wants, and needs;

- ask and answer questions;
- tell stories; and
- share feelings.

AAC apps may be used for a variety of purposes, including:
- primary source for communication,
- temporary versus permanent solution,
- backup system for other device,
- communication training, and
- learning.

AAC may be used in many different settings, such as:
- school,
- home,
- playground,
- over the phone,
- restaurants, and
- stores.

AAC may be used with many different people, including:
- family,
- teachers and therapists, and
- friends.

Careful consideration needs to be given to the following:
- **Language representation:** What is the best way to present words and concepts? Photos of people and items in a person's environment, video, abstract images, and printed words can be used.
- **Visual display:** How many images or words should be presented at one time? Should a person have a finite group from which to select or should the person be able to scroll for more choices and produce novel messages?
- **Word selection:** What needs to be communicated? There is much more to life than just naming objects. As mentioned earlier, comments, requests, and questions are an integral part of communication.
- **Communicative intent:** Does the individual need to be externally motivated to communicate? How is the student currently communicating and what further skills need to be developed?
- **Communication abilities:** What are the language, speech, cognitive, and social skills of the person?
- **Implementation plan:** It is important to consider the following:

- How will the device be configured? What are the strategies for successful implementation of the device into daily routines?
- How much support is available?
- Who will continue to update the device as the needs of the individual change?
- Even if families do turn to communication professionals for comprehensive assessments, the speech-language pathologists are confronted with a number of dilemmas. How should the availability of these new products change the traditional AAC assessment and intervention process? Should professionals wait for research to take place as new products become available prior to using them in their professional practices?

- A plan should be established for customization of the app or device, training and therapy, and follow up.
- Everyone involved needs to appropriately reinforce communication attempts, model the use of the device, and expand newly learned skills into the home and daily routines.

ONLINE RESOURCES

The following online resources may be helpful for individuals trying to learn more about this exciting but complicated field of AAC during this transformation.

AAC Institute
http://www.aacinstitute.org/
- This is a compilation of helpful AAC resources.

AAC Language Lab
https://aaclanguagelab.com/
- Prentke Romich Company provides helpful information on language stages and teaching resources. It offers solutions in support of language development. There are many materials designed for teachers, parents, and speech-language pathologists.

AAC TechConnect
http://www.aactechconnect.com
- A site filled with great suggestions and resources on AAC.

Janice Light and Kathy Drager

http://aackids.psu.edu

- This is a very helpful website with suggestions about early intervention strategies to help children learning language. Several informative videos are included.

Learning Paths

http://www.dynavoxtech.com/implementation-toolkit/learning-paths

- This site offers many wonderful resources by Dynavox.

Spectronics AAC Apps

http://www.spectronicsinoz.com/blog/tools-and-resources/aac-apps-speaking-appropriately

- This is a very comprehensive blog by Jane Farrall, an SLP and special educator in Australia who is passionate about literacy, assistive technology, and AAC.

The International Society for Augmentative and Alternative Communication (ISAAC)

https://www.isaac-online.org

- As stated on its website, ISAAC's mission is to promote the best possible communication for people with complex communication needs.

The SETT Framework

http://www.joyzabala.com

- Joy Zabala's model to be used in the collaborative decision-making process in all phases of assistive technology and AAC selection and implementation.

YAACK, Augmentative and Alternative Communication (AAC) Connecting Young Kids (YAACK)

http://aac.unl.edu/yaack

- The purpose of this organization is to help families and professionals with issues using AAC with children at various ages and stages of communication ability.

SIMPLE COMMUNICATION ITEMS WITHOUT VOICE OUTPUT

Symbols, pictures, and words can be used to facilitate communication. Books, picture communication charts, calendars, maps, and other items may be able to help augment expressive communication. Many of these products can be purchased in multiple languages. These simple communication items are often most effective when they are personalized. In addition to being used to augment communication, they can be used to practice new verbal skills. These items generally support face-to-face interactions and are slow.

There are some mobile devices that can be used to print out communication boards, such as the following.

Custom Boards Premium
by Smarty Ears
http://www.smartyearsapps.com/service/custom-boards
- Select from more than 11,000 built-in symbols or add your own pictures and use one of many templates provided to create activities and games, devices and switches, signs and labels, grids and boards, schedules and calendars, and worksheets.
- iOS
- $39.99

ProxTalker App
by Logan Technologies
http://www.logan-technologies.co.uk/proxtalker-app
- This app uses the symbolstix library with more than 15,000 symbols so that users can develop customized visual communication boards, task lists, schedules, and more. Multiple template options are offered.
- iOS
- Free

DIRECT-SELECT, ONE-LEVEL, VOICE OUTPUT COMMUNICATION DEVICES

Direct-select, one-level, voice output communication devices are relatively simple devices with which messages are created on the device or are already programmed and activated by pressing a button to select a picture, word, or phrase. These communication devices include everything from talking picture frames and talking photo albums available to more specialized tools. Numerous alternatives are available from AbleNet (http://www.ablenetinc.com), Enabling Devices (http://EnablingDevices.com), and Dynavox Mayer-Johnson (http://Mayer-Johnson.com).

Direct-select, one-level, talking communication devices can be used as a stepping stone to determine readiness for more complex devices. These "talking" devices use pictures and words that the person who programs the device determines are most important for the individual to communicate. When the user selects the picture, a prerecorded word or phrase is played aloud on the device. By selecting a picture or word, users may be able to "verbalize" basic needs and wants in real life and practice the utterances in therapy. If the user is unable to initiate use of these tools, the devices are often helpful for the communication partner. The combination of the picture and voice output helps comprehension.

GoTalk

by Attainment Company

http://www.attainmentcompany.com

- Several versions are available, with varying numbers of pictures. Multiple layers of pictures can be recorded.
- The price range is from $12 for GoTalk One to $599 for GoTalk 32+, which also has scanning capabilities.

LiveScribe Pen

by LiveScribe

http://www.livescribe.com

- This pen records all that is said as the user writes. The recorded audio can be replayed by tapping directly on the special dot paper with the pen that recorded the audio. Creative users can use this pen to create talking flash cards, schedules, communication boards, and memory books by recording speech on the special paper and then cutting up the paper and putting them on index cards or in a scrapbook.
- 2 GB Sky Wi-Fi Smartpen: $169.95 for 200 hours of audio (varies by audio quality setting)

Talking Photo Albums

by Attainment Company

http://www.attainmentcompany.com/talking-photo-album

- Talking photo albums enable the user to press a section on the bottom of an album page and hear spoken words corresponding to a picture made by the person who programmed it.
- $39

MOBILE DEVICE APPS WITH STATIC DISPLAY

Answers: YesNo

by Simplified Touch

http://www.simplifiedtouch.com/SimplifiedTouch/YesNo.html

- This is a great app for using two large customizable buttons to convey a message.
- iOS
- $1.99

GoTalk Now

by Attainment Company Inc.

http://www.attainmentcompany.com

- This app is my top pick for this category. There are three styles of communication pages: Standard, Express, and Scenes, in which invisible hotpots can play speech, music, and videos. There is a helpful page wizard and the ability to back up books via Dropbox and to share books with others who have the app.
- iOS
- $79.99

My First AAC

by Injini

http://www.injini.net

- Animated icons with sign language for words and phrases. Icons organized by categories that reflect children's natural speech development. More than 250 related words and phrases to express frequently used ideas.
- iOS
- $24.99

Scene Speak

by Good Karma Applications

http://www.goodkarmaapplications.com/scene-speak1.html

- This app provides a framework for images to be edited with hotspots to which sound and text or links to another scene can be added.
- iOS
- $9.99

Sounding Board

by AbleNet

http://www.ablenetinc.com/Assistive-Technology/Communication/SoundingBoard

- Create customized boards using AbleNet symbols or photos.
- iOS
- Free (in-app purchases)

TapSpeak Sequence

by Ted Conley

http://tapspeak.com/drupal/sequence

- This app is a modernized version of the step-by-step communication device. It is one in a series.
- iOS
- $29.99 (in-app purchases available)

DYNAMIC COMMUNICATION DEVICES, APPS, AND SOFTWARE

Devices with dynamic display capabilities automatically change the picture displays and corresponding messages using internal hyperlinks. Novel messages can be communicated through sequential selection of pictures or words. Dynamic display can be found on dedicated communication devices that have been around for a long time as well as on newer AAC apps on touch screen mobile devices.

Dynamic communication devices use either digitized or synthesized speech to assist with communication. Digitized devices use recorded speech for the messages that will be heard by the communicators. Synthesized communication devices translate text into electronic speech. In recent years, the synthesized voices have sounded much less robotic than in the past. There are many more natural voices from which to choose.

A comprehensive review of dedicated communication devices is beyond the scope of this book. Please refer to the following websites or the websites listed earlier in this chapter for additional information.

- http://www.dynavoxtech.com
- http://www.gusinc.com
- http://www.prentrom.com
- http://www.saltillo.com

DYNAMIC COMMUNICATION MOBILE APPS

I have included only a small number of the many apps that are available. These products are full of extremely helpful features. It is extremely important that knowledgeable teams support the implementation of AAC apps.

Alexicom Tech

by Alexicom Tech

http://www.alexicomtech.com

- This Internet-based AAC system uses core words and phrases and has more than 1,200 premade pages and 1–100 cells per page with unlimited linking. It can be configured online or on the device. Scanning and switch access is available. There is automatic server backup.
- Android, iOS, Mac, and Windows
- One user for 1 month: $40

Assistive Express

by Assistive Apps

http://www.assistiveapps.com

- This app offers text to speech (words that are typed are spoken aloud), word prediction, high-quality voices, and the ability to save phrases.
- iOS
- $24.99

Autismate

by SpecialNeedsWare

http://autismate.com

- This app features visual scenes that can be customized to the needs of the user, a grid-based AAC sentence builder, video modeling,

visual schedules and stores, a content library, and is GPS-enabled so that certain scenes appear based on physical location.
- iOS
- $149.99

Avaz for Autism
by Invention Labs
http://www.avazapp.com
- This is a full-featured AAC app with three graded picture vocabularies and core words. It uses SymbolStix images.
- Android and iOS
- $99.99

GridPlayer
by Sensory Software International
http://www.sensorysoftware.com/gridplayer
- This includes more than 24,000 symbols (Widgit and SymbolStix), word list grids, and quick response buttons for answering questions.
- iOS
- Free (need to purchase the computer software to modify the contents)

Lamp Words for Life
by Prentke Romich Company
http://aacapps.com/lamp
- This is a fully featured AAC app designed with motor planning and language acquisition principles in mind. The app includes core and fringe words, developmentally progressive vocabulary files, and much more.
- iOS
- $299.99

Predictable
by Therapy Box Limited
http://www.therapy-box.co.uk
- This is not a symbol-based app like the others presented in this section. It is a text-to-speech app offering social media integration, word prediction, switch access, and category/phrase banks.
- Android and iOS
- $159.99

Proloquo2go

by AssistiveWare

http://www.assistiveware.com/product/proloquo2go

- This fully featured AAC app is the leader of the pack. It has had quite a few improvements recently. The app is now accessible with adaptive switches, offers multiple voices, several core word vocabularies maximized for different grid layouts and levels, and includes 14,000 SymbolStix images. It is now available for social sharing with e-mail, Facebook, SMS, and Twitter from inside the app. Educational tutorials are available at httpwww.assistiveware.com/support.
- iOS
- $219.99

Sono Flex

by Tobii Technology

http://www.tobii.com/en/assistive-technology/global/products/software/sono-flex

- This fully featured AAC app combines core and topic-based vocabularies in a unique way. There are more than 50 premade context vocabularies. Several versions are available.
- Android, iOS, and Windows
- $99.99

Speech Tree

by Global Augmentative Communication Innovators

http://speechtreeapp.com

- This is a AAC app combined with an interactive learning program. It features fully customizable pages, 20 different lessons to teach receptive and expressive skills, more than 5,000 photos and symbols, and can be used by multiple individuals.
- iOS
- $169.99

Talking Tiles

by Mozzaz Corporation

http://www. mozzaz.com/index.php/products/talkingtiles

- This app is very customizable, includes a library of more than 50,000 symbols, and supports more than 30 different language, voice, and accents. It also supports remote programming.
- Android, iOS, and Windows
- Free trial, then $10 a month

Tap Speak Choice AAC
by Ted Conley
http://tapspeak.com/drupal/choice

- This app can be used as a two-button communication board to complete page sets for speech generation. It uses Pixon symbols. Pages for word endings are included for grammatically correct sentences.
    - There are many accessibility options for a wide range of motor and vision options.
    - There are antistimming modes as well as modes for button preview, touch, tap, detect touch on release, scanning and switches.
    - Pages can have one to 56 buttons and can be linked.
    - Forty languages and 88 voices are supported.
- iOS
- $169.99

TouchChat
by Silver Kite
http://www.touchatapp.com

- This is an excellent fully featured AAC app that can be customized online. Very helpful video tutorials are available at http://touchchatapp.com/support/videos.
- iOS and Windows
- $149.99 (in-app purchases available)

CELL PHONES

Cell phones have become increasingly important in today's society. Pay phones are rare and often do not function. People with difficulty communicating should carry a cell phone if they travel alone in the community so that they can call others who are familiar with their situation for help as needed. If they are unable to talk, the caller ID can signal to the recipient of the call who they are, and that person can bear the conversational burden by asking yes/no questions or using other helpful communication techniques.

For individuals who have relatively preserved cognitive abilities, sequencing skills, and manual dexterity, features of smartphones can augment communication abilities. Phones now come equipped with cameras, video chat capability, text messaging, speech recognition, and more.

With a bit of imagination and creativity, mobile phones can become powerful communication and cognitive assistants. The following useful features provide examples:

- **Address book:** Helpful for recalling names of people.
- **Calendar:** Helpful for remembering and organizing information and for referring to names, dates, and places in conversation.
- **Still and video cameras:** Provide an effective way to communicate by sending a person a picture of a situation, a person, a place, or an event or speaking live while seeing each other.
- **GPS:** Many of the newer phones can be configured so that GPS functions are enabled. It is possible to locate a phone to monitor a child's location or find a misplaced device. iPhones have an app called Find My iPhone and Android phones use an Android Device Manager (ADM) feature. With both of these sytems, it is possible to locate, track, wipe clean of information, or have the phone loudly ring—all from a web browser.

Many apps offer text to speech so that users can type and have their words said aloud over the phone. For more information, please refer to the text-to-speech section in Chapter 9: Technology and Strategies to Improve Written Expression.

Many apps are available for meeting online and seeing each other as you speak. For more information, please check out these products:

- **Google Hangout** (http://www.google.com/hangouts): Google Hangout has become very popular with students. Users need to have a free Google+ account. E-mail correspondence can be upgraded to chat and then to a Hangout by clicking on a photo in the chat list.
- **Skype** (http://www.skype.com): Voice and video calls as well as messages that are sent to anyone else on Skype are free. Conference calls with three or more people are available for a fee. Instant messaging, file transfer, and screen sharing are available.
- **ooVoo** (http://www.oovoo.com): Free video chats are possible with up to 12 people at a time who have a free account. Users can use text chat and send files.

ACCESSIBLE CELL PHONES

People with physical, communication, or cognitive disabilities frequently find the use of a standard mobile phone with small buttons difficult to use. The following websites may help you find the appropriate type of phone.

- http://www.fireflymobile.com
- http://www.etoengineering.com
- http://www.just5.com

CHAPTER 6

TECHNOLOGY AND STRATEGIES TO
IMPROVE AUDITORY COMPREHENSION

It is devastating when a person is unable to understand spoken language. Young children first develop their listening skills prior to developing other skills such as speaking, reading, and writing. Listening and understanding play a crucial role in our daily lives. In conversation, we translate speech into meaningful language. As we listen, we decode and identify meaningful words effortlessly.

In many ways, technologies can help children who have a hard time understanding what is said to them. They can both compensate for and provide drill and practice for activities to improve the comprehension of words, directions, and conversations. The use of technology also empowers students with auditory challenges to increase the time spent practicing specific comprehension skills.

In this chapter, cutting-edge assistive technologies are highlighted that can be used to enhance auditory comprehension. As with verbal expression, a multimedia approach using sound, text, and pictures helps with understanding.

People with auditory comprehension and processing deficits may demonstrate the following characteristics:

- a short attention span,
- signs of distractibility,
- oversensitivity to sounds,
- misinterpretation of what is said to them,
- confusion of words,

- poor vocabulary,
- need for frequent repetition,
- inability to follow directions,
- difficulty with speech and verbal expression,
- poor reading comprehension, and
- are learning English as their second language.

In children, a central auditory processing disorder (CAPD) occurs when the ear has intact acuity, but the brain has difficulty processing the information. Auditory information breaks down somewhere beyond the ear. Because the majority of early learning is auditory, a weakness in how language is processed can lead to delayed development with reading. Auditory processing is a critical component to reading success. More information about CAPD can be found at these sites:

- http://www.asha.org/public/hearing/disorders/understand-apd-child.htm,
- https://www.nidcd.nih.gov/StaticResources/health/healthy hearing/tools/pdf/audiprocdis.pdf, and
- http://www.ncld.org/types-learning-disabilities/adhd-related-issues/auditory-processing-disorders/auditory-processing-disorder-by-age-group.

It is rare, but I have seen quite a few children who have suffered strokes and head injuries, and even though they had developed language normally, they are left with a language-based, auditory comprehension deficits referred to as "receptive aphasia." As with other language modalities, working to improve auditory comprehension is a complex task. The reasons for the difficulty need to be thoroughly evaluated so that the strategies and therapeutic interventions are appropriate. A person may appear not to understand, but the problem may be complicated by a variety of other issues, such as problems with hearing, attention, processing, and memory. Prior to the selection of products, it's essential to analyze the major obstacles of comprehension and figure out what is needed to improve it. Professional help from a speech-language pathologist who specialized in pediatric language evaluations should be used whenever possible. A thorough evaluation of receptive language skills and the best course for improving them is a complex process.

The following technology features are useful for improving auditory comprehension:

- option to play back recordings at a slower speed,
- option to repeat stimuli said aloud,

- controlled vocabulary to what is known or access to one-click digital dictionary,
- controlled context so student is familiar with and interested in the content, and
- controlled length of material being listened to.

TREATMENT APPROACH

When helping children who have difficulty understanding what is said to them, it is helpful to find other ways to enhance the message being said, such as the following:

- Make sure to have the full attention of the listener prior to speaking.
- Communication partners such as parents, teachers, therapists, and peers need to be shown how to use the environment to support the message. Gestures, pictures, written words, calendars, clocks, objects, and actions should be used.
- Speak more slowly, face the listener, and speak clearly.
- Minimize external distractions such as the TV and other extraneous visual and auditory stimuli.
- Provide multisensory cues. People do best when they can see a word, hear a word, and perhaps touch an object.
- Present words in their natural context. For instance, try to talk about food items while in the kitchen, or have a calendar to refer to while talking about dates.
- Avoid shouting from another location.
- Engage in activities that help people become more aware of the sounds around them, listen for patterns of sounds, discriminate differences between sounds, and become more observant of letter sounds (phonemes).

TECHNOLOGY TO HELP IMPROVE AUDITORY COMPREHENSION

Different apps and software programs provide different ways of assisting with or compensating for auditory comprehension challenges. The websites for each described product are given to provide you with information that is more detailed regarding versions of the software, networking ability, preferred operating systems, and availability of online tutorials or demos. The prices written in this guide are generally for an individual home full version of each item. These prices will undoubtedly change, but they are included to give a ballpark estimate.

Many of the apps listed in the verbal expression and reading comprehension chapters of this book can also be used to help improve auditory comprehension.

COMPREHENSION OF SOUNDS

With some of these apps, there is a sound and the user selects the sound. For others, the parent, therapist, or teacher can play a sound on a touch device without the patient seeing what they select, and then the patient has to find it. Some work on sounds of animals or objects; others work on identifying letter sounds.

Fido's Magic Soundbox
by Pixel Interactive
http://littlelearningtots.com/wp/ipad-app
- iOS
- $.99

Kids Animal Toys (Real Sounds)
by XigXag Interactive
https://play.google.com/store/apps/details?id=com.XigXag.KidsAnimal&hl=en
- Android
- Free

Sound Beginnings
by Preschool University
http://preschoolu.com/iPhone-iPad-Apps.html#SoundBeginnings
- iOS and Mac
- Free

Sound Touch
by SoundTouch
http://www.soundtouchinteractive.com
- Android and iOS
- $4.99

Touch the Sound
by Innovative Mobile Apps
http://www.alligatorapps.com
- iOS
- Free

COMPREHENSION OF WORDS

These apps provide effective ways for students to practice understanding words. Many are customizable so that pictures can be added, cueing hierarchies established, or desired words selected.

ABA Receptive by Noun
by Kindergarten.com
http://www.kindergarten.com
- This is one in a series of apps.
- iOS
- $1.99

Auditory Processing Studio
by Virtual Speech Center
http://www.virtualspeechcenter.com/Resources/auditory_processing_studio_app.aspx
- iOS
- $29.99

Bitsboard
by GrasshopperApps.com
http://www.grasshopperapps.com/apps/bitsboard
- Words can be studied in a selected category using the flash card portion, then practiced using the photo touch section of this app.
- iOS
- Free

Comprehension TherAppy

by Tactus Therapy Solutions

http://tactustherapy.com/apps/comprehension

- This is very customizable and appropriate for older students who don't respond to younger looking apps. It is also part of the Language TherAppy app.
- iOS
- $24.99

Photo Touch Concepts

by GrasshopperApps.com

http://www.grasshopperapps.com/apps/photo-play

- This is one in a series of apps.
- iOS
- $.99

Word Slapps Vocabulary

by Zorten Software

http://zorten.com/slapps/wordslapps

- iOS
- $4.99

COMPREHENSION OF PHRASES AND SENTENCES

Be sure to check out the options in these apps. Most allow the user to customize the content of the stimuli.

Auditory Processing Studio

by Virtual Speech Center

http://www.virtualspeechcenter.com/Resources/auditory_processing_studio_app.aspx

- iOS
- $29.99

Auditory Workout

by Virtual Speech Center

http://www.virtualspeechcenter.com/Resources/auditory_workout_app.aspx

- iOS
- $19.99

Describe it (SLP)
by Synapse Apps
http://pocketslp.com/our-apps/describe-slp
- iOS
- $9.99

EasyConcepts
by Easy Speak Enterprises
http://easyspeakenterprises.com/apps
- iOS
- $4.99

Fun With Directions
by Hamaguchi Apps
http://hamaguchiapps.com/Fun_with_Directions.html
- iOS
- $15.99

Let's Talk Following Instructions
by Let's Talk Apps
http://www.letstalkapps.ie/whydoesitwork.html
- iOS
- $1.99

Lexico Cognition
by Pappy GMBH
http://www.pappy.ch/apps/lexico-cognition-for-ipad
- iOS
- Free (full version is $9.99 with in-app purchase)

One Step Two Step
by Synapse Apps
http://pocketslp.com/our-apps/one-step-two-step
- iOS
- $19.99

Picture the Sentence
by Hamaguchi Apps
http://hamaguchiapps.com/Picture_the_Sentence.html
- iOS
- $9.99

Questions2Learn

by Speech Pups

http://www.speechpups.com

- iOS
- $9.99

Describe With Art

by Virtual Speech Center

http://www.virtualspeechcenter.com/Resources/describe_with_art_app.aspx

- iOS
- $9.99

COMPREHENSION OF PARAGRAPHS AND SHORT STORIES

Many of the apps and products listed in the chapter for reading comprehension can be used for listening comprehension. If there is text that is read aloud, practice sessions can be created by taking away access to the written text and testing for comprehension of the material that is said aloud.

BrainPOP Featured Movie

by BrainPop

http://www.brainpop.com/apps/landing

- There is a different movie every day with comprehension questions.
- Android, Chrome, iOS, and Windows
- Free

Listening Master

by LingualNet

http://lingual.net/game/listening-master

- iOS
- $2.99

FUN APPS TO PRACTICE COMMUNICATION

It's helpful to take turns giving and listening to directions for others to move items in the app.

. . . .

English Adventures for Kids
by WireCloud
http://www.easylanguageforkids.com
- iOS
- $3.99

ClickySticky
by Merge Mobile
http://mergemobile.com/apps/clickysticky
- Android and iOS
- $1.99

Face Changer
by Scoompa
http://www.scoompa.com
- Android
- Free

Make My Face
by Conversation
https://itunes.apple.com/us/make-my-face/id559313985?mt=8
- iOS
- $.99

My PlayHome
by MyPlayHome
http://www.myplayhomeapp.com
- Android, iOS, and Windows
- $3.99

These are helpful computer programs to work on improving auditory comprehension skills:

Hear Builder®: Following Directions
by SuperDuper Inc.
http://www.hearbuilder.com/followingDirections

- HearBuilder is a series of educational software programs designed to help students improve their listening and memory skills.
- Each HearBuilder focuses on specific areas of learning with multiple levels. Concepts taught are in five primary areas: basic directions, sequential directions, quantitative and spatial directions, temporal directions, and conditional directions.
- Mac and Windows
- $69.95 for the home edition

No-Glamour® Auditory Processing Interactive Software
by Carolyn LoGiudice
http://www.linguisystems.com/products/product/display?item=10370

- This product is an auditory perceptual training program designed for use by children with learning or communication disabilities. The program improves auditory processing skills in the areas of: auditory reception, following directions, recognizing absurdities, phonological awareness, details, exclusion, identifying the main idea, problem solving, riddles, and comprehension.
- Lessons can be customized for multiple students.
- Pre- and posttest results, session responses, and student progress can be recorded and documented.
- Mac and Windows
- $43.95

FREE WEBSITES WITH LISTENING ACTIVITIES

Most of these sites were developed to teach English as a second language, but can be very helpful for individuals with auditory comprehension and processing disabilities.

- **Randall's ESL Cyber Listening Lab** (http://www.esl-lab.com)
- **EnglishClub Listening** (http://www.englishclub.com/listening)
- **Easy World of English** (http://easyworldofenglish.com/readings/readings.aspx?c=2f1dbe126863ea88)

- **ESOL Courses** (http://www.esolcourses.com/content/topics menu/listening.html)

LONG-DISTANCE COMMUNICATION

Communicating on the phone is difficult if someone has a hard time with auditory comprehension. Several solutions are available.

- **Text:** If the individual can read, try sending text messages or using e-mail or fax to communicate.
- **Images:** It is very helpful to supplement verbal messages that are difficult to understand with nonverbal support. Many people who can't speak on the phone, which just offers auditory stimuli, do much better when they can see the person with whom they are speaking or when the person on the other end of the phone can show rather than tell them to what they are referring. Try these free apps or websites:
  - **Facetime**, Apple (http://www.apple.com/mac/facetime), iOS
  - **Google Hangouts**, Google (http://www.google.com/+/learn more/hangouts), Android, iOS, Mac, and Windows
  - **Skype** (http://www.skype.com/en), Android, iOS, Mac, and Windows

ASSISTIVE LISTENING DEVICES

Assistive listening devices (ALDs) include a large variety of devices designed to improve comprehension in specific listening situations. Some are designed to be used with cochlear implants or hearing aids with a T-switch, while others are designed to be used alone. Assistive listening devices improve the listener's ability to hear by making the desired sound stand out from the background noise. Being able to hear can have a major impact on a person's ability to participate in social, academic, and work situations. Additional information can be found on these websites:

- **Assistive Listening Device Systems** (http://www.alds.com)
- **Hearing Loss Web** (http://www.hearinglossweb.com)
- **American Speech-Language-Hearing Association** (http://www. asha.org/public/hearing/treatment/assist_tech.htm)
- **Ablenet** (http://www.ablenetinc.com/Assistive-Technology/Assist ed-Listening-Devices)
- **Harris Communications** (http://www.harriscomm.com)

CAPTIONING

CLOSED CAPTIONING

Closed captions contain text that is hidden within normal television broadcasts and DVDs. A television with the built-in caption decoder chip or an external decoder is needed to make the captions visible. It can typically be turned on or off by viewing the menu of options available on the TV. There's no special service to subscribe to in order to receive the captions. Captioning is made free for all viewers by the television and home video industries, and with the support of grants and donations. This multisensory experience of watching captioned TV has been shown to improve significantly the reading skills of children. In addition, people learning English can improve their language and vocabulary skills and adults with auditory comprehension deficits can improve their comprehension of the spoken material.

REAL-TIME CAPTIONING

Real-time captioning currently takes place when a person types what is said into a stenotype machine. The machine is connected to a computer with software that translates the shorthand into words in caption formats and standard spellings. It is now becoming possible to tape lectures and presentations, then to use voice recognition software to transcribe what is said. As technology advances, this procedure has enormous potential for helping people with communication and cognitive deficits. However, the accuracy of voice recognition software with dictation is inconsistent. Free software for closed captioning may be found at the National Center for Accessible Media website (http://ncam.wgbh.org/webaccess/magpie). The following websites may be helpful:

- **National Association of the Deaf** (http://www.nad.org/issues/technology/captioning/cart)
- **Collaborative for Communication Access via Captioning** (http://ccacaptioning.org/faqs-cart/)
- **National Institute on Deafness and Other Communication Disorders** (http://www.nidcd.nih.gov/health/hearing/caption.asp)
- **Described and Captioned Media Program** (http://www.dcmp.org)

CHAPTER 7

TECHNOLOGY AND STRATEGIES TO
IMPROVE READING COMPREHENSION

READING CHALLENGES

Many students have difficulty reading and do whatever they can to avoid it, but research studies show that children need to practice reading every day in order to improve their reading skills. This situation often sets the stage for much unhappiness at home and in the classroom. Impaired reading ability can be the result of a learning disability, language delay, cognitive deficit, or visual and perceptual problems. Fortunately, there are now many technology tools and strategies to help improve as well as compensate for struggles with reading.

Reading is a complex task. To effectively help children who are having difficulty reading, you need to understand where the problems arise. Reading issues can stem from difficulties with auditory perception, visual perception, or language processing. Many barriers exist. The text may be too small or the page too cluttered. Some individuals have challenges paying attention while reading or decoding words. Others may be able to understand individual words, but read slowly and have difficulty processing what they read. Individual words may make sense, but challenges arise when they have to synthesize the information in order to find the main idea, identify implied information, paraphrase the content, or locate desired information. People who have difficulty with reading may present with many different scenarios. They may:

- show poor ability to sound out words;

- have overall poor literacy skills;
- be able to read aloud well, but show poor comprehension;
- understand the content, but not be able to remember it;
- go through the motions of "reading" but, when tested, show little comprehension of what they appeared to read;
- get visually lost on the page or be unable to see the words;
- show slow processing time, which makes it difficult to keep up with reading demands at school or work, or may prevent reading for pleasure;
- demonstrate the ability to read basic information, but be unable to process complex material; or
- speak another language.

There are a number of strategies that have been around a long time that can be used to improve reading without technology. Here are a few:
- Sound the word out slowly.
- Break the word into parts.
- Read the word aloud.
- Skip the word and come back to it.

These conventional tips don't help everyone. Many students end up relying on having others read aloud to them to help with comprehension or they try their best to read, but err in their efforts.

DYSLEXIA

Dyslexia is a reading comprehension disorder that involves phonological processing. Students often respond favorably to timely and appropriate intervention. For more information about dyslexia, visit:
- The International Dyslexia Association (http://www.interdys.org/InsInt.htm)
- The National Center for Learning Disabilities (http://www.ncld.org/types-learning-disabilities/dyslexia/what-is-dyslexia)

HELP FROM PROFESSIONALS AND WEBSITES

Tools needed to improve and compensate for reading challenges of different etiologies vary. As with other communication and literacy challenges, specialists should be consulted whenever possible to maximize progress. Successful use of assistive devices and drill-and-practice software depends on:

- pairing the appropriate tools with the individual based on his or her deficits,
- training the individual to use the product or device, and
- providing appropriate support to resolve problems and help integrate new learning into everyday routines.

Many professionals are able to assist in the treatment of reading challenges. Speech-language pathologists, occupational therapists, reading specialists, special education teachers, educational therapists, and vision specialists are trained to work on particular approaches to improve reading.

It is important that students who struggle with learning to read and who are suspected of having visually-based deficits be evaluated and treated by a vision specialist.

Research has shown that there is a close relationship between language development and literacy skills. Be sure to involve speech-language pathologists early whenever language development is delayed. There is quite a bit of research concerning the potential causes of reading difficulties and the most effective treatment options. It's been proven that people who have difficulty reading have a better chance of comprehending and retaining the content of written material with a guided reading approach and if they can simultaneously see the words and hear them read aloud. The following are some helpful online resources:

- **National Institute of Child Health and Human Development** (http://www.nichd.nih.gov/health/topics/reading/conditioninfo/pages/work.aspx)
- **Readwritethink** (http://www.readwritethink.org/parent-afterschool-resources)
- **LD OnLine** (http://www.ldonline.org)
- **TechMatrix** (http://www.techmatrix.org)

HELPFUL FEATURES OF TECHNOLOGY TO SUPPORT READING

In recent years, many assistive reading technologies have become included in devices to help make them more universally accessible. There are also software products and apps that are especially helpful in compensating for and/or improving reading.

In order to select effective technologies to assist with reading, consider which of the following features would be helpful for the person with the reading deficit. Assistive technology tools can help by:

- reading aloud, highlighting, and enlarging text that is printed on the screen;
- changing the format of the text to make it easier to view;
- converting printed text from a paper or book into editable text to help with studying, to enable the material to be read aloud on a computer, or to be converted to audio files; and
- saying words aloud and giving definitions.

Drill-and-practice apps, software, and websites can enable the user to:
- improve auditory-perceptual skills and phonics;
- pair text with graphics for users who can interpret pictures, but not the printed word;
- encourage students to read text aloud and record what they say to improve reading skills;
- work on visual tracking and scanning to improve reading fluency; and
- provide text for drill and practice with effective strategies to facilitate comprehension and analysis.

READING ALOUD, HIGHLIGHTING, AND ENLARGING TEXT ON A SCREEN

There are now many free options available that people can benefit from when reading a document, their e-mail, or an online newspaper or webpage. The options may differ depending on the type of device or browser you are using for online access as well as the operating system and version. It is now possible to have text that is on a screen enlarged and read aloud without purchasing additional software. It is often included in accessibility features of operating systems and browsers. Here are some websites for the most popular operating systems, browsers, and software with more information:

Microsoft
- MS Windows (http://www.microsoft.com/enable)
- MS Office 2010 (http://www.microsoft.com/enable/training/office 2010/default.aspx)

Apple
- http://www.apple.com/accessibility/

Google/Android
- http://www.google.com/accessibility/products

Text size: Most people who have difficulty reading do better with larger font size. Most browsers now have customizable text size and many mice, keyboards, and touch screens can also be used to change the font size.

Highlighting: Research has shown that people do best not when the text is only read aloud, but when the words are highlighted as they are spoken and as the person views the text. It is ideal when the sentence is highlighted in one color and the individual words in another color.

Reduced clutter: It is helpful when ads and other distracting visual content are removed for reading. Online text may also be "saved for later" when offline. These products will work with many types of operating systems. Check out the following websites to explore options for your phone, tablet, or computer.

- **Readability** (http://www.readability.com)
- **Dolphin Reader** (http://dolphin.com/add-ons/tools/dolphin-reader)

Keyboards/Mice: Many keyboards and mice offer options for zooming in and enlarging online text that most users are not aware exist. To make text larger on a PC, try "Ctrl +"; "Ctrl −" will decrease the size. For a Mac, use the Command + or Command − to change the size. On some mice, after selecting the "control" or "command" button on the keyboard, you may be able to scroll up or down on the mouse to change the font size.

There are also quite a few programs on the market to assist people with low vision. It's beyond the scope of this guide to review them all. Additional information can be found on the following websites:

- **The Low Vision Gateway** (http://www.lowvision.org)
- **Enablemart** (http://www.enablemart.com)
- **Independent Living Aids** (http://www.independentliving.com)

TEXT TO SPEECH

It is becoming increasingly mainstream to have devices that are able to read text aloud from the screen. This is referred to as text to speech. This multisensory input is very helpful for struggling readers. It can help improve attention, focus, processing, retention, and proofreading. The reader can usually determine the speed that the text is read aloud and may have a choice of different voices. They are much more natural sounding now than in the past.

There are quite a few text-to-speech (TTS) products on the market that offer features beyond what the accessibility features of operating systems and browsers offer. This software may include the following features:

- the ability to control auditory features and visual presentation;

- the ability to save the documents as auditory files;
- options, such as voice, rate of speech, highlighting, and screen display, that can be individualized, depending on the product;
- text that can be read back one letter, word, line, sentence, or paragraph at a time;
- words that can be magnified as they are read aloud; and
- the ability to work with e-mail, websites, and multiple file formats.

More sophisticated products with TTS can also provide additional help with reading, writing, and studying by enabling the student to:
- electronically highlight sections of text in different colors,
- take notes by typing or by voice,
- prepare outlines,
- create flash cards and other study materials,
- use word prediction,
- summarize written material,
- read only highlighted sections, and
- skip to the bookmarked section of text.

There are several ways to access the text to speech option on a Mac. Here is one way to do it:
- Open the System Preferences by selecting the Apple menu on the top left of the screen.
- Select the Speech icon.
- Click the "Text to Speech" tab.
- Choose your preferred voice and speed. Click on the play button to hear a sample.
- You can decide which two keyboard buttons to press to access this feature. I usually set it at "command" and "s."
- When you want something read aloud you just highlight the text and press the two keyboard buttons.

iPad/iPhone: If you have updated to at least a fairly recent operating system for your iDevice, you should be able to take advantage of built-in text to speech. It is called "speak selection" and has a highlighting option. Here is how I access it:
- Select "Settings" and "General."
- Look on the right side and scroll down to select "Accessibility."
- Under the "Vision" section, you can select "Text" to increase the font size.

- Go to "Speak Selection" and turn it on. Select your desired dialect and speaking rate.
- Turn on the "Highlight Words" option.
- When you have text you'd like read aloud, hold your finger on the text to select it; a bubble appears.
- If the content highlighted is your desired text to read aloud, select "speak." If not, then move the small blue balls around to select the text.

PCs: Narrator is a screen reader that has been available in many iterations of Windows. It is more geared toward helping individuals with low vision than for people with language-based reading issues. Speak is a built-in text-to-speech feature of Word, Outlook, PowerPoint, and OneNote. For more information, check out this website: http://office.microsoft.com/en-us/word-help/using-the-speak-text-to-speech-feature-HA102066711.aspx#_Toc282684835.

There are many options available with text to speech. Some software is downloaded onto your computer and then accessed when online. Other products are useful for specific web browsers. The free versions tend to have fewer features and more robotic sounding voices. I typically try to first figure out the type of material that needs to be read aloud (e.g., websites, documents, books, e-mail), view the price, consider the available technologies as well as the ease of use, and then sample the voices used as well as features needed to help make the most appropriate selection. I have included some of my top picks below:

- **Natural Reader** by NaturalSoft Ltd. (http://www.naturalreaders.com)
- **Balabolka** by Softpedia (http://www.softpedia.com/get/Science-CAD/Balabolka.shtml)
- **Google Chrome-Speakit!** by Google (https://chrome.google.com/webstore/detail/speakit/pgeolalilifpodheeocdmbhehgnkkbak?hl=en)
- **FoxVox** by Mozilla Firefox (https://addons.mozilla.org/en-us/firefox/addon/foxvox)
- **TextAloud3** by NextUp (http://www.nextup.com)
- **Universal Reader Plus** by Premier Literacy (http://www.readingmadeEZ.com)

OPTICAL CHARACTER RECOGNITION

Optical Character Recognition (OCR) enables a user to scan printed material into a computer or device. The software converts the "image" to text, so a text-reading program can read the written material to the user. Different programs use different scan and OCR engines. Certain programs work best with certain scanners. Also, some work better than others with replication of the image, scanning speed, form-filling capabilities, and study skills. This technology has advanced remarkably in recent years.

Software with OCR and TTS:

- **Kurzweil 3000™** by Kurzweil Educational Systems (http://www.kurzweiledu.com)
- **WYNN Literacy Software** by Freedom Scientific (http://www.freedomscientific.com/LSG/index.asp)

The apps listed below will read multiple formats aloud or offer OCR and TTS.

Mobile OCR Free

by Smart Mobile Software

http://www.smartmobilesoftware.com/mobile-ocr.html

- Android and iOS
- Free

Premier Talking Reader

by Kenneth Grisham

http://www.readingmadeez.com/products/iPad_PremierTalkingReader.html

- Premier Talking Reader can read text in multiple formats and offers Dropbox integration.
- iOS
- $14.99

TextGrabber + Translator

by Abbyy

http://www.abbyy.com/textgrabber

- Android and iOS
- $5.99

vBookz PDF Voice Reader US

by Mindex International Ltd.

http://www.vbookz.com/V1/vBookz_Support.html

- vBookz PDF Voice Reader offers text to speech in PDF files.
- The app uses a font for people with dyslexia named dyslexie.

- There are video instructions for accessing text in Google Drive, Dropbox, iBooks, and Safari
- iOS
- $4.99

Voice Dream Reader- Text to Speech
by Voice Dream LLC
http://www.voicedream.com
- Voice Dream Reader includes many helpful features for reading PDF files, ebooks (in epub format), MS Word documents, and additional formats.
- The app integrates with Bookshare, Dropbox, Google Drive, and Evernote.
- It can fast forward by sentence, paragraph, page, chapter, or time and export highlighted text and notes.
- iOS
- $9.99

Web Reader (TTS Web Browser)
by Baek Pack
- Android
- $.89

ADVANCED TEXT READERS WITH READING, WRITING, AND STUDYING TOOLS

The software programs listed here are ideal for students who need reading as well as writing support. They offer a wide variety of effective and well-researched literacy supports. Be sure to take the time to view their websites for additional information. The products in this list have been around for quite a while and are used often in school systems.

Classroom Suite
by Intellitools
http://www.intellitools.com/classroom-suite.html
- Mac and Windows
- $345

Kurzweil 3000™

by Kurzweil Educational Systems

http://www.kurzweiledu.com/Kurzweil-3000-v13-windows.html

- Mac and Windows
- $1,395

Literacy Productivity Pack

by Premier Literacy

http://www.readingmadeeasy.com/products/lpp.html

- Mac and Windows
- $249.95

Read and Write Desktop

by Text Help

http://www.texthelp.com/North-America/readwrite-family

- Mac and Windows
- $645

Read:OutLoud

by Don Johnston

http://www.donjohnston.com/readoutloud

- Mac and Windows
- A single computer license is $249.

SOLO Literacy Suite

by Don Johnston

http://www.donjohnston.com/solo

- Mac and Windows
- A single computer license is $699.

WYNN Reader

by Freedom Scientific

http://www.freedomscientific.com/LSG/pruducts/wynn.asp

- Mac and Windows
- $99 per license

PICTURE-BASED, TALKING WORD PROCESSORS

People with severe reading deficits who are unable to use text-based word processors to read are often able to benefit from picture-based, talking word processors. These programs typically offer speech feedback, symbols, or pictures to support text and on-screen grids. These programs enable the therapist, teacher, or parent to create reading activities specifically suited to individuals, incorporating as many or as few pictures and sound support as needed. The following software is for use on a computer:

- **Clicker** by Crick Software (http://www.cricksoft.com), offers wide range of curriculum and accessibility support, $300, Mac and Windows
- **Communicate: Symwriter** by Dynavox Mayer-Johnson (http://www.mayerjohnson.com/communicate-symwriter-windows), $223.99, Windows

ALTERNATIVE READING FORMATS, INTERACTIVE TEXTBOOKS, AND WEBSITES WITH ACCESSIBLE BOOKS FOR CHILDREN

There are more and more ways to read a book other than the traditional paper format. Text-to-speech software can read books aloud and allow for bookmarks, annotations, and comments. Audiobooks are narrated by a human voice. Braille books are provided for people who are blind. Interactive talking books can be used to improve reading skills.

An increasing number of books as well as textbooks are now available in e-text format. There are many benefits to interacting with books that are in a digital format to increase comprehension and retention of information as well as speed of processing for all students, including those with language and literacy challenges. Benefits include:

- **The ability to change the appearance of the text.** The way the reader sees the text can have a profound impact on comprehension. Cluttered pages, with little white space and small print, make reading more difficult. With e-text, it's often helpful to enlarge the font and increase the color contrast of the text and background to make on-screen reading easier.
- **Use of pictures and video.** Visual supports can enhance comprehension.
- **Interactive images and activities.** Learning is enhanced when students are more actively engaged in the learning process.

- **Bookmarking capability.** It's very helpful when students can save where they are in a book and then pick up where they left off on the same or another device.

There are many sources where you can download or view books in alternative formats, and many are free. In my experience, many families who can tremendously benefit from these resources do not know that they exist. Most of these organizations also offer apps for mobile devices. Bookshare and Learning Ally should be considered for all students who struggle with reading.

Bookshare

http://www.bookshare.org
- Bookshare is free for all U.S. students with a documented "print disability." It is available by paid subscription for others with print disabilities who wish to join.
- It offers a searchable online library of approximately 202,000 digital books, textbooks, and periodicals.
- Families are able to obtain their own membership, but certain textbooks are only available for school-based accounts.
- The digital downloads can be read aloud in a browser, from mobile devices using free apps, or from a Mac or PC computer with software that is provided by Bookshare or other software already used by the student.
- Their app is referred to as Read2Go on iOS devices and Go Read on Android devices.
- $75 for individuals without a print disability

Learning Ally

https://www.learningally.org
- This organization has evolved from Reading for the Blind and Dyslexic. It provides access to more than 75,000 narrated books. Compatible with most computers and mobile devices.
- Parts of their website are now more focused on parents' questions and linking the educator to the family.
- New features include supports for parents and teachers referred to as Parent Ally and Teacher Ally. Teacher Ally enables teachers to assign audio to students, and it stores and provides information on student usage, which it can convey in a written report.

- Their app for mobile devices is called Learning Ally and at the time of this update is only available for iOS devices.
- Some titles are available with Voicetext, a human voice that is synchronized with the text which is viewable on iOS devices and the ReadHear software.
- $49 per year

Accessible Book Collection
http://www.accessiblebookcollection.org
- This is a subscription-based service that provides high-interest reading material at a low reading level. It offers detailed information on the reading level for each title.
- The primary audience is youth with learning disabilities.
- Intellipics and Clicker formatted picture books are available.
- Tools are available so that the text size, color, and spacing of their eBooks can be changed.
- Individuals are eligible if they have a documented disability that prevents them from reading standard print effectively.
- $49.95 per year

Browser Books
http://staff.prairiesouth.ca/~cassidy.kathy/browserbooks/index.htm
- This is a website for beginner readers with engaging, colorful photographs.
- Online books are sorted by level and subject.
- After selecting a book, children can read it on their own or click on words to have them read aloud in natural-sounding children's voices.
- Readers turn the page by clicking on a triangle.
- Free

iBooks
by Apple
http://www.apple.com/ipad/built-in-apps/#ibooks
- It includes the iBookstore.
- Users can type notes and bookmark sections and they will be saved and synced to iCloud.
- There are a variety of viewing options and the text size and font can be changed.
- Books can be viewed that include audio and video.

- It includes a built-in dictionary and supports multitouch interactive features in books.
- Library books which are in the ePub electronic book format (and Digital Rights Management-free) can be added to iTunes and synced to the device.
- Most PDF documents can be saved in iBooks.
- iOS
- Free

International Children's Digital Library
http://www.childrenslibrary.org

- THE ICDL Foundation's goal is to create a collection of books that represents outstanding historical and contemporary books from throughout the world.
- The ICDL collection includes more than 4,600 books in 61 languages.
- There are also books available for iPad/iPhone.
- Free

Crack the Books iTextbooks
by Mobile Education Store
http://www.mobile-educationstore.com

- Crack the Books is a new interactive textbook series for upper elementary students using interactive enhancements and accessibility features to enhance learning and engagement.
- It includes built-in supports and assessments as well as the ability to track progress.
- Prices vary.

Librivox
http://librivox.org

- This site provides audio recordings of books in the public domain.
- Books can be downloaded to a computer, listened to on iTunes, or burned to a CD.
- Free

Online Leveled Reading Library
http://www.raz-kids.com

- Users can benefit from listening for modeled fluency, reading for practice, recording their reading, and checking comprehension with the quizzes.

- Learning A-Z licenses are sold on a per classroom basis, which is what a parent should select if ordering for home use. Each teacher who has paid and registered can use the license with up to 36 students in one classroom.
- Contact the company for pricing information.

Overdrive Media Console

http://omc.overdrive.com

- This app enables users to read and listen to eBooks and audiobooks from their library on many different devices.
- Users can customize their reading experience with bookmarking and customization tools and a built-in dictionary.
- Android, Blackberry, iOS, Kindle, Mac, Nook, PlayBook, and Windows
- Free

Project Gutenberg

http://www.gutenberg.org

- More than 42,000 free eBooks to read on your Android, iPad, iPhone, Kindle, Sony Reader, PC, or other portable device.
- No fee or registration is required.
- All books are free in the United States because their copyright has expired.
- An online book catalogue is available and users can browse by author, title, language, or recently posted.
- Books are available in many languages.

Start-to-Finish Online Accessible Library

by Don Johnston

http://www.donjohnston.com/products/stfonline/index.html

- Books that are available in the Start-to-Finish Library described below are available online.
- Android, iOS, Mac, Windows
- $429 unlimited access per site per year

Start-to-Finish Library and Core Content

by Don Johnston

http://www.donjohnston.com/stflibrary

- An accessible book collection developed for older elementary and early adolescent students reading below grade level.

- There is a wide selection of age-appropriate narrative chapter books written at two readability levels and delivered in three media formats—paperback, audio, and computer.
- Users practice reading fluently and with comprehension using multiple text and electronic supports.
- The computer books offer a comprehension quiz after each chapter and work on reading fluency.
- Mac and Windows
- Each computer book is approximately $29.99.

Storia

http://store.scholastic.com/microsite/storia/home

- Storia provides favorite titles from Scholastic Books, current eBooks, read-to-me-books, and enriched books which offer contextual learning activities, games, quizzes, and author interviews.
- Storia offers an integrated dictionary, reference tools (highlighter and note taker), reading reports, personalized bookshelves, and connectivity at home and school.
- Five free eBooks are available for download for Windows PC, iPad, Kindle Fire and Android tablets.

Storyline Online

http://www.storylineonline.net

- This site offers video streaming of stories read aloud by actors as readers follow along with text.
- Suggested related activities are also included.
- Free

Tar Heel Reader

http://www.tarheelreader.org

- This site includes a collection of easy-to-read books on a wide variety of topics.
- Each book can be speech-enabled and accessed using multiple interfaces, including touch screens, the IntelliKeys with custom overlays, and one to three switches.
- Appropriate for beginning readers of all ages, including adolescents.
- Many books are available in multiple languages.
- Free

Tumblebook Library

http://tumblebooks.com

- This is an online collection of animated, talking picture books for young children.
- It offers a variety of Apple apps.
- Contact the company for pricing information.

ADAPTED ONLINE NEWSPAPERS

News-2-You

http://www.news-2-you.com

- A weekly Internet-based picture newspaper using SymbolStix that features current events and other articles of interest.
- There are four editions: simplified, regular, higher, and advanced.
- Two communication boards can also be downloaded each week with pertinent vocabulary.
- Articles about world news are displayed on an interactive Google map.
- Many downloadable activity pages are included as well as web-based games.
- Students can follow along as words are highlighted.
- There is a News-2-You app that is a collaborative offering between AssistiveWare and N2Y for iOS devices. One edition is included for free.
- $149 for a single subscription per year

NewsCurrents

http://www.newscurrents.com

- NewsCurrents is a current events newspaper with accompanying discussion guides for classroom use.
- It's written on three levels of difficulty and is available online or on DVD.
- Read to Know is a weekly nonfiction reading program based on current events. Subscribers receive 34 issues a year, each one filled with timely news and feature stories. Each story is written on a level students can understand and includes background information, photos, and other teaching images like maps. Student users read the stories on the computer and then test their knowledge

with comprehension quizzes and thought questions at the end of each story.

- A subscription includes a weekly issue (for 34 weeks of the year) with images corresponding to five or six stories in that week's news.
- $269 for a year-long subscription

BookBox
http://www.bookbox.com
- This resource is most appropriate for children.
- It includes downloadable Flash stories that are digitally narrated with simple animation and streaming text across the bottom.
- It synchronizes the text, audio, and visual media to create an educational and entertaining reading experience.
- The reader sees whole phrases, and the letters go from white to red as the words are spoken.
- The stories are available in multiple languages.
- Many stories are available for download for $2.99 each, while CDs with several stories are approximately $12.99.

PORTABLE EBOOK READERS

The use of portable eBook readers has gained momentum in mainstream society. eBooks can be wonderful assistive technology tools that, when paired with effective instruction and guidance, can greatly help individuals who have reading challenges.

Below is a list of popular eReaders. An online search will reveal many more. One important feature to look for to help individuals with reading challenges is their ability to read the books while the eReader uses text to speech. Please be sure to keep in mind that in some cases, the publishers of the books will not permit this to happen. The books being read aloud with text to speech sound very different from audiobooks, which have people reading the books aloud rather than a computer (which in many cases can sound very much like a human). It's also helpful to be able to access the widest variety of books. The ePub format is needed to read library books. Some readers are able to be used in direct sunlight, while others use background lighting and have a glare in direct light. Additional features that some of these devices offer are color and the ability to watch videos and listen to music.

- **iPad Mini** (http://store.apple.com/us/ipad)
- **Kindle** (http://www.amazon.com/kindlefamily)
- **Nook** (http://www.barnesandnoble.com/NOOK)

eReaders are gaining in popularity due to these improving features:

- People can store many books, magazines, and newspapers in a very small, lightweight device that is easy to carry.
- Some devices can read aloud the books using text to speech or recorded voices such as the Kindle.
- New technology makes reading very easy on the eyes and easier to read in direct sunlight.
- Prices have dropped.
- They now have a longer battery life.
- They are easier to use.
- Books can be purchased directly from the device.
- Some devices are compatible with book formats for library books and books from sources such as BookShare.
- Apps such as the Kindle app are now available for computers, tablets, and smartphones with a wide variety of operating systems so that books can be read from more than one device.
- Users can typically change the font size.
- Many offer bookmarking and annotation features.
- Some allow readers to share books such as the Nook.

This world of more affordable, fully featured eReaders is changing fast and will continue to improve. There can now also be a social component to reading. More and more hybrids are being developed which function as eReaders but also allow the user to access the Internet and offer word processing capabilities. On some of the devices such as the Kindle, it is possible for users to use social networking sites such as Twitter and Facebook to post their notes and the text as they highlight while reading.

APPS FOR LISTENING TO AUDIOBOOKS

Audiobooks are pleasant to listen to because they are professionally narrated. In order to help improve comprehension and reading skill for students, I highly recommend that if students choose to listen to audiobooks, they also obtain the print copy of the book and read along as they listen. Many can be found in libraries and most bookstores. Here are two additional online resources:

- **Audiobooks** by Cross Forward Consulting, LLC (http://www. blog.travelingclassics.com)
- **Audiobooks from Audible** by Audible, Inc. (http://www.audible. com)

INTERACTIVE BOOK APPS

For young children as well as reluctant readers, book apps are very engaging and help bring books to life. Hundreds are available. Below are listed some of my top picks, which offer opportunities for learning and discussion and which are enjoyable for kids to read. Features may include:

- read yourself or "read to me" option with professional narration,
- text highlighting as a child hears the word,
- explore pages and touch-activated animations, and
- realistic page turning (swipe your finger or click on a corner).

There are quite a few sites that review digital interactive books. One site I have found helpful when searching for apps for older struggling readers is Digital Storytime (http://www.digital-storytime.com).

Here are some of my favorite developers that offer affordable interactive books as well as a few of my top picks for books that are available on multiple platforms:

- **Oceanhouse Media** (http://www.oceanhousemedia.com), Android and iOS
- **Age of Learning** (http://www.abcmouse.com/apps), Android and iOS
- **Bacciz** (http://bacciz.com), iOS
- **Brush of Truth** by Story Bayou Inc. (http://www.storybayou.com), a wonderful story for middle school age students who are reluctant readers; Android, iOS, Kindle, Windows; $1.99
- **Houghton Mifflin Harcourt** (http://www.hmhco.com/kids-teens/digital-and-mobile-learning), storybooks as well as interactive textbooks; Android and iOS
- **SmallPlanet** (http://www.smallplanet.com/apps), Android and iOS
- **Mindshapes** (http://www.mindshapes.com), iOS
- **MeeGenius Inc.** (http://www.meegenius.com), Android and iOS
- **Electric Eggplant** (http://www.electriceggplant.com), Android and iOS
- **Disney** (http://disneybookapps.com/category/apps), Android and iOS
- **Penguin Leveled Readers** (https://itunes.apple.com/us/app/penguin-leveled-readers/id624700709?mt=8), iOS
- **PlayTales, S.L.** (http://www.playtalesbooks.com/en/), Android and iOS
- **8interactive Limited** (http://8interactive.com), Android and iOS
- **Reading Rainbow** (http://www.rrkidz.com/), iOS and Kindle Fire
- **Storia** (http://store.scholastic.com/microsite/storia/home), Android and iOS

- **StoryPals** (http://ericsailers.com/storypals.html), a reading comprehension app designed by a speech-language pathologist; iOS; $19.99

READING ALOUD HANDHELD DEVICES

There are an increasing number of affordable portable devices, in addition to some of the eReaders mentioned earlier in this chapter, that can read aloud to help individuals who are unable to read.

. . . .

AnyBook Anywhere
by Franklin Electronic Publishers
http://www.franklin.com/anybook-amywhere#sthash.AMOpysØsd.dpbs
- The AnyBook Reader is a device that looks like a pen, but functions more like a digital recorder when used with a special collection of stickers.
- While in the record mode, the person recording touches a sticker with the pen, then records a message. Each sticker has a unique code which is then linked with the audio file. When the listener is in play mode, he touches the sticker and listens to the recording play back.
- Recordings can take place online and be stored virtually in a library and shared with others.
- No text is involved except that the device is supposed to be placed on pages on a book so that a child can hear a parent reading the book aloud to them.
- The stickers can be used creatively to help users sequence steps in a task, listen to instructions, or provide reminders.
- $79.99

LeapReader
by LeapFrog
http://www.leapfrog.com
- This company produces a number of very engaging and interactive devices to encourage learning.
- LeapReader offers a wide variety of activities to practice sounding out words, reading sentences out loud, writing letters of the alphabet as well as numbers, and improving listening skills with audiobooks and music.
- LeapReader Read and Write Book Bundle costs $35.99.
- Add-on content is available.

CHAPTER 8

DRILL-AND-PRACTICE TECHNOLOGY TO
IMPROVE READING SKILLS

INTERACTIVE SOFTWARE AND APPS WITH ACTIVITIES TO IMPROVE READING

There are many computer software programs and mobile apps that use a drill-and-practice approach to improve reading skills. Many of these programs:

- are interactive and engaging,
- offer tasks at a variety of reading levels,
- can be customized,
- provide immediate feedback regarding the accuracy of the response, and
- document performance.

Keep in mind that new versions of software and apps are frequently being released and features are frequently changed. It is important to review websites for more up-to-date and in-depth analyses of product comparisons. Please note that online programs will not work on all devices. iOS devices are not compatible with interactive websites that were programmed using Flash. Sites using HTML5 coding should work fine. The best way to figure out compatibility is just to give it a try. In addition to the items in this chapter, there are many more wonderful online programs that offer interactive reading activities listed in Chapter 13: Interactive Websites and Games to Promote Communication, Literacy, and Learning.

SOFTWARE AND ONLINE PROGRAMS

Between the Lions
by PBS Kids
http://pbskids.org/lions
- This site offers many easily accessible activities that contain words and phonics. Each of the games provides visual and auditory help for users with cognitive and learning challenges.
- Free

BrainPro
by Scientific Learning
http://www.brainsparklearning.com
- This program combines the Fast ForWord® software with a professional online consultant to help students improve their ability to read by working on the building blocks to reading in an enjoyable way. The tutors monitor the user's progress and provide guidance to parents or teachers.
- Mac and Windows
- Contact providers on the website for pricing.

Click N Read Phonics
by Click N Kids
http://www.clicknkids.com
- This online reading curriculum uses engaging graphics and includes 100 kindergarten through third grade reading lessons.
- Check website for prices of different packages.
- Online

Earobics
by Cognitive Concepts
http://www.earobics.com
- Each level is specially developed to help students build critical literacy skills, including recognizing and blending sounds, rhyming, and discriminating phonemes within words.
- Mac and Windows
- $99 (home version)

Edmark Reading Program–Software Version

by Edmark

http://www.donjohnston.com; http://www.enablemart.com;
http://www.prufrock.com

- Using a whole word approach, this program teaches recognition and comprehension of words with built-in instructions, audio cues, and feedback.
- The Level 1 software version teaches 150 words chosen from the Dolch Word List for first-grade readers, as well as "-s," "-ed," and "-ing" endings, capitalization, and punctuation.
- Level 2 teaches 200 words, including compound words, and reviews and reinforces words learned in Level 1. At 10-word intervals, a review and test activities are provided.
- Mac and Windows
- $254.99 per level

Explode the Code® Online

by CurriculaWorks

http://www.explodethecode.co

- This is a comprehensive phonics-based curriculum for grades K–4 that has been available (although there have been changes) for more than 30 years. The online version helps students build the essential literacy skills needed for reading success: phonological awareness, decoding, vocabulary, comprehension, fluency, and spelling.
- Online
- $65 per year

Fast ForWord

by Scientific Learning Corporation

http://www.fastforword.com

- This is a reading intervention program provided by trained specialists to help students who are struggling and reading below grade level. It was developed specifically for students with learning issues. It offers programs that feature a sequenced learning environment that advances cognitive skills in the context of appropriate reading skills.
- The program is based on research showing that most literacy-based learning problems result from the brain's difficulty processing rapidly changing auditory information.
- Mac and Windows
- Contact company for pricing.

Goodwill Community Foundation International

http://www.gcflearnfree.org

- Gcflearnfree.org is an interactive website designed to help teach functional skills through a variety of free online activities. There is an excellent section on reading.
- Free

HearBuilder Phonological Awareness

by Super Duper Publications

http://www.hearbuilder.com/phonologicalAwareness

- This software gives students a systematic way to improve auditory and phonological awareness skills.
- Students use the phonics activities to earn band members and instruments for their rock band.
- Users complete increasingly difficult sound awareness tasks and work to demonstrate understanding in nine areas: Sentence Segmentation, Syllable Blending, Syllable Segmentation, Rhyming, Phoneme Blending, Phoneme Segmentation and Identification, Phoneme Deletion, Phoneme Addition, and Phoneme Manipulation.
- Mac, Online, and Windows
- $69.95 for home edition

Hop, Skip and Jump

by Sound Reading Solutions

http://www.soundreading.com/hsj-information.php

- This software is designed for young children learning to read. It develops preword, word, and sentence reading, as well as printed and spoken word fluency. Twenty activities develop phonemic awareness, sound discrimination, auditory attention, and memory for comprehension.
- Mac, Online, and Windows
- $99.95 for online version

Lexercise

by Mind inFormation

http://www.lexercise.com

- Lexercise is a web-based program that is customized by a supervising clinician for children ages 6–16 with language-literacy disorders. It teaches alphabetic phonics through individualized, sequential, multisensory gamelike exercises.
- Online
- Contact the company for pricing information.

Lexia Reading Software
by Lexia Learning Systems
http://www.lexia4home.com/content/lexia-materials
- Lexia offers several programs for different ages that build strength in phonemic awareness, sound-symbol correspondence, decoding, fluency, phonics, and vocabulary.
- Lexia Early Reading is for ages 4–6, Lexia Primary Reading is for ages 5–8, and Lexia Strategies for Older Students is for ages 9–adult.
- The software is based on the Orton-Gillingham method of reading remediation. A web-enabled version offers a school-to-home connection.
- Spanish and English directions support ESL learners.
- Mac, Online, and Windows
- $174.95 for a one-year subscription

Literactive
http://www.literactive.com
- Literactive offers free online reading material for preschool, kindergarten, and first-grade students. The program is comprised of carefully leveled animated guided readers, comprehensive phonics activities, and supplemental reading material. A complete phonemic and syllabic breakdown of every word in the stories is provided, enabling each child to decode the written text alone or in small classroom groups.
- ESL versions for the reading material are available for download. Starting with initial nursery rhymes, it moves through prereading activities, alphabet awareness, letter sounds, short vowels, CVC word blending, initial blends, long vowels, and many phonics-based activities that are critical for developing early reading skills.
- Online
- Free

Merit Software
http://www.meritsoftware.com
- This company's products cover the core reading skills through interactive exercises that use contextual help with text-to-speech technology.
- They offer a variety of products categorized by grade level as well as subject.
- Reading Comprehension Booster Online, $45 (home user)

- Developing Critical Thinking Skills Online, $45 (home user)
- Mac, Online, and Windows

Mimio Home Reading Programs
by HeadSprout
http://www.mimio.com/en-NA/Products/Mimio-Home-Reading-Software.aspx

- Mimio offers a wide range of reading tools for the classroom and home that can be used on a computer or mobile device, such as MimioSprout™ Home Reading Software for Beginning Readers and MimioReading™ Home Software for Reading Comprehension.
- MimioSprout Home Reading Software for Beginning Readers teaches basic component skills and strategies necessary for reading, such as phonemic awareness (the sounds within words), print awareness, phonics, sounding out, segmenting, and blending, and are practiced in a fun, self-directed manner. The second half of the program focuses more on reading vocabulary, fluency, and comprehension, while still teaching more sounds and sight words. $99
- MimioReading Home Software for Reading Comprehension includes 50 30-minute online lessons that teach students strategies to master the four main components of comprehension: finding facts, making inferences, identifying themes and the "main idea," and learning vocabulary in context. $99

Reader Rabbit Series
by The Learning Company
http://www.broderbund.com

- I used this company's products all the time when my children were young. They offer a wide variety of affordable mainstream software for children. Activities involve working through puzzles, games, stories, and more with Reader Rabbit while practicing reading and language skills. Reader Rabbit apps are also available.
- iOS, Mac, and Windows
- $9.99–$19.99

Reading Assistant
by Scientific Learning
http://www.scilearn.com/products/reading-assistant

- This software uses oral reading practice, voice recognition, intervention strategies, and quizzes to help students improve reading fluency, vocabulary, and comprehension. It "listens" to a person as he or she reads aloud and highlights words that are read aloud incorrectly and models appropriate answers as needed.

- Mac and Windows
- This software is available from trained specialists.
- Contact Scientific Learning for pricing.

Reading Comprehension Level 1 Interactive Software
by Abigail Hanrahan and Catherine McSweeny
http://www.linguisystems.com/products/product/display?itemid=10554

- This program uses short passages with engaging screen designs. There are five readability levels and 11 comprehension skills.
- Mac and Windows
- $41.95

Reading Detective Software
by The Critical Thinking Company
http://www.criticalthinking.com

- This software develops the analysis, synthesis, and vocabulary skills needed for reading comprehension. There are several different versions of this software targeted for different age groups and abilities. The activities help users understand reading concepts such as drawing inferences, determining cause and effect, and using context clues to define vocabulary.
- Three levels are provided. At each level, users read and analyze short pieces of literature, both fiction and nonfiction. They then answer multiple-choice questions, citing evidence to support their answers.
- Mac and Windows
- $24.99 for a single-user CD.

Reading Remedy
by Sound Reading Solutions
http://www.soundreading.com/remedy-information.php#video2

- This program was created for older students who are reading at or above the third-grade level. It strives to install excitement for reading with dynamic content which lets the student take charge while teaching all the skills needed to read, including critical listening skills, phonemic awareness, and fluency.
- Mac, Online, and Windows
- The online single user version is $99.95.

Rocket Reader

by Rocket Reader

http://www.rocketreader.com

- Several products are available to increase reading speed, comprehension, and reading stamina. This software works to improve reading speed and comprehension with a combination of exercises, flash training, speed training, practice reading, and timed tests.
- The software runs only on Windows, but the online versions work on Linux, Mac, and Windows.
- $139 for 3 months.

Route 66 Literacy

http://www.route66literacy.org

- This reading and writing program is for older students who are beginner readers. It provides high-interest activities for students who are accompanied by more experienced readers on the computer with the support of a "teacher tutor." This program was created by literacy experts at the University of North Carolina at Chapel Hill in partnership with Benetech.
- Online
- Free

Spotlight on Reading & Listening Comprehension Levels 1 and 2

by Linguisystems

http://www.linguisystems.com

- This software includes more than 60 narrated stories and 480 multiple-choice questions. Users listen to and read aloud with each story and its follow-up questions and answers. Narrated audio can be turned on and off at any time. Each story screen includes a full-color picture to help visual learners attach meaning to the text. Users can review the text of the story as they answer comprehension questions.
- Mac and Windows
- $59.95 for each level.

RAZ-Kids Online Leveled Reading Library

http://www.raz-kids.com

- This is a game-based reading website and leveled-reader program. Students receive points for doing things, such as finishing a book or completing a quiz, and move up in the ranks, eventually to Fleet Admiral. They also earn points to purchase items to add to their

Raz Rockets. The students benefit from listening for modeled fluency, reading for practice, recording their reading, and checking comprehension with quizzes.

- Online
- $99.95 for a one-year subscription for 1–36 students.

Scholastic

http://www.scholastic.com

- This website offers very helpful reading resources for both families and educators. There are printables as well as online activities by grade and subject. Go to the "Kids" sections and then the "Family Playground."
- Online
- Free
- Scholastic's Storia app is available on multiple devices for interactive eBooks, Android, iOS, and Windows.

Starfall.com

by Starfall

http://www.starfall.com

- This reading program consisting of more than 30 online activities. The reading lessons are divided into four sections: ABC's, Learn to Read, It's Fun to Read, and I'm Reading.
- The ABC's introduces students to letter sounds.
- Learn to Read teaches students how letters are combined to create words.
- It's Fun to Read uses learning activities to introduce simple sentences.
- I'm Reading uses simple plays and folk stories to increase student's reading fluency.
- Starfall offers a wide variety of products, including a pre-K home curriculum and an app for iOS and Android.
- Online
- Free

Time4Learning

by Time4Learning

http://www.time4learning.com

- This is an online educational program that teaches preschool through eighth-grade curriculum using a combination of animated lessons, interactive activities, and reinforcing worksheets.

- The reading programs teach and improve phonemic awareness (reading readiness), phonics, reading fluency, vocabulary, and comprehension.
- The language arts program teaches reading comprehension, fluency, vocabulary, grammar, pronunciation, punctuation, word roots, literary analysis, and critical thinking.
- Online
- $19.95 per month for the first child

MOBILE APPS TO IMPROVE LANGUAGE-BASED READING DEFICITS

The following mobile apps focus on phonics and words.

Abby Sight Word Games & Flash Cards
by 22Learn LLC
https://www.22learn.com/action_sight_words_games_flash_cards.html
- One in a series of apps
- Android and iOS
- $1.99

ABC Alphabet Phonics
by GrasshopperApps.com
http://https://itunes.apple.com/us/app/abc-alphabet-phonics-preschool/id415071093?mt=8
- One in a series of apps
- iOS
- Free

ABC Phonics Word Family
by Abitalk Inc.
http://www.abitalk.com
- One in a series of apps
- Android and iOS
- Free

ABC Pocket Phonics
by Apps in My Pocket
http://www.appsinmypocket.com/pocketphonics/index.html
- iOS
- $2.99

Auditory Analysis (USA Accent)
by Talking Talk
http://talkingtalk.co.za
- Android
- $6.40

Bob Books
by Learning Touch
http://www.bobbooks.com/reading-apps-for-kids
- One in a series of apps
- iOS
- $3.99

First Words Deluxe
by Learning Touch
http://www.learningtouch.com
- One in a series of apps
- iOS
- $4.99

Interactive Alphabet ABCs
by Pi'ikea St.
http://www.piikeastreet.com/apps/interactive-alphabet
- iOS
- $2.99

iTouchiLearnWords: Speech & Language Skills
by Staytoooned
http://www.staytoooned.com
- Android and iOS
- $1.99

Kids ABC Phonics
by Intellijoy
http://www.intellijoy.com/games/kids-abc-phonics
- One in a series of apps
- Android and Blackberry
- $2.99

Letter Reflex

by Binary Labs

http://www.dexteria.net

- Helps users overcome letter reversals
- iOS
- $1.99

Monkey Word School Adventure

by THUP Games, LLC

http://www.thup.com/portfolio/monkey-wordschool-adventure

- One in a series of apps
- Android and iOS
- $1.99

My First 1,000 Words

by Innovative Mobile Apps

www.alligatorapps.com

- One in a series of apps
- $1.99

SightWords Pro

by 24 x 7 digital

http://www.24x7digital.com/appstore/SightWordsPro

- One in a series of apps
- iOS
- $1.99

Sight Words for Reading

by Rock n Learn

http://rocknlearn.com/html/apps.htm

- One in a series of apps
- Android and iOS
- Free

Sound Beginnings

by Preschool University

http://www.preschoolu.com/iPhone-iPad-Apps.html#SoundBeginnings

- One in a series of apps
- iOS and Mac
- Free

Starfall Learn to Read
by Starfall Education
http://more.starfall.com/info/apps/starfall-education.php
- Android and iOS
- $2.99

Super Why!
by PBS Kids
http://www.pbskids.org/mobile/super-why.html
- Android, iOS, Kindle tablet and Nook tablet
- $2.99

Word BINGO
by ABCya.com
http://www.abcya.com
- One in a series of apps
- iOS
- $.99

THE FOLLOWING MOBILE APPS FOCUS ON SENTENCES

Many of the apps described in Chapter 6: Technology and Strategies to Improve Auditory Comprehension, especially those involving following directions, can also be helpful for reading comprehension practice when the sound is turned off.

Language Empires
by Smarty Ears
http://www.smartyearsapps.com/service/language-empires
- To work on reading, turn off the sound.
- iOS
- $24.99

Rainbow Sentences
by Mobile Education Store
http://mobile-educationstore.com/apps.sentence-structure-apps/rainbow-sentences
- iOS
- $7.99

Sentence Reading Magic
by Preschool University
http://www.preschoolu.com/iPhone-iPad-Apps.html#SentenceReading Magic
- One in a series of apps
- iOS
- Free

Sight Words Sentence Builder
by Sierra Vista Software
http://www.k5stars.com/video_demos/Sentence_Builder_Game_demo_video.php
- iOS and Windows
- $1.99

WHQuestions
by Smarty Ears
http://www.smartyearsapps.com/service/whquestions
- iOS
- $9.99

THE FOLLOWING MOBILE APPS FOCUS ON PARAGRAPHS AND SHORT STORIES

Aesop's Quest
by NRCC Games
https://itunes.apple.com/us/app/aesops-quest/id442928041?mt=8
- iOS
- $.99

Kids Reading Comprehension
by Angela Reed
https://itunes.apple.com/us/app/kids-reading-comprehension/id494472230?mt=8
- One in a series of apps
- Android and iOS
- $.99

One Minute Reader
by Read Naturally
http://readnaturally.com/products/omrInfo.htm
- One in a series of apps
- iOS
- Free

Reading Champion
by TextHelp
http://www.texthelp.com/noth-america/readingchampion
- iOS
- $2.99

Reading Comprehension Camp
by Smarty Ears
http://www.smartyearsapps.com/service/reading-comprehension-camp
- iOS
- $19.99

Reading Comprehension for Kindergarten and First Grade
by Abitalk Inc.
http://www.abitalk.com
- One in a series of apps
- Android and iOS
- $2.99

Reading Comprehension Solar System for 5th Grade
by Abiltalk Inc.
http://www.abitalk.com
- One in a series of apps
- iOS
- Free, in-app purchases

StoryPals
by Expressive Solutions
http://ericsailers.com/storypals.html
- iOS
- $19.99

SOFTWARE FOR VISION-BASED READING DEFICITS

Many student have difficulty processing what they see. This is referred to as a visual processing disorder. It is very different from a visual acuity problem. More information can be found at:

- **National Center for Learning Disabilities** (http://www.ncld. org/types-learning-disabilities/adhd-related-issues/visual-processing-disorders)
- **LD Online** (http://www.ldonline.org/article/6390)

People with visual deficits often:

- reverse, invert, and misalign letters;
- avoid reading;
- have difficulty copying written material and have messy papers;
- reread and skip lines;
- complain that print blurs while reading;
- turn their head or close an eye while reading;
- hold their paper at odd angles to read; and
- have difficulty recognizing an object or word if only part of it is shown.

People who have visual-perceptual deficits or low vision can often benefit from the use of text-to-speech or screen-reading software, which was described in Chapter 7: Technology and Strategies to Improve Reading Comprehension. Many programs highlight words and sentences as they are read aloud and work to help improve visual-perceptual skills. The highlighting can help with scanning and tracking the written words.

There are quite a few interactive apps which can help to improve visual perceptual skills. Some are game-based while others are more drill-and-practice in nature. Many of these apps will be listed in Chapter 12: Interactive Programs to Improve Cognition, Learning, and Memory.

CHAPTER 9

TECHNOLOGY AND STRATEGIES TO
IMPROVE WRITTEN EXPRESSION

The use of traditional blackboards is disappearing from classrooms and interactive whiteboards are taking their place. This increasing use of multimedia in classrooms to teach and enable students to show what they know is very helpful for students with special needs, but most schools remain primarily text-oriented. This is a major problem for significant numbers of learners who struggle with writing. There are many students who have difficulty with one or more aspects of written language. In schools, it is very common to see these students using a scribe or struggling with attempts to use a complex speech recognition program. In my experience, there are many other solutions that should be considered when attempting to determine the most appropriate assistive technology solution for a student with special needs.

As with other aspects of language and cognition, help from a trained professional should be used when possible to help select and implement the appropriate strategies and resources to facilitate progress. It is very important that children develop competent writing skills. The inability to express themselves in written form effectively can have far reaching negative implications academically and in terms of self-esteem. Fortunately, there are now many assistive technologies as well as drill-and-practice apps and software that can help to develop written expression skills.

We are in the midst of a huge transition and varying opinions from a wide variety of experts about what tools are best to use to help students who struggle with literacy. Products and features are changing rapidly.

Budgets and time to learn about new technologies are limited. New types of computers, web-based technologies, and mobile devices are emerging at an unprecedented pace. Assistive technology specialists are struggling to keep up and it then takes a while for this information to reach families and students in schools.

There is a movement toward the use of cool new mobile devices and cloud-based technologies. By using less expensive, more mainstream options, more students are able to benefit. There are many more students who struggle with writing than who receive specialized support.

In my experience, it is rare that students in mainstream public classrooms readily accept the notion of using computers in the classroom for writing supports if other students are not using technology. Most classrooms don't have enough computers for everyone and students don't want to be different than others and carry laptops that can be heavy and cumbersome from class to class or to their homes. More portable and socially accepted mobile devices are increasingly becoming the go-to solution. It is much better for students to use a less effective technological solution than only use pen and paper, but it is important that we don't lose sight of the many well-researched, fully featured, computer-based technologies that are available.

SKILLS NEEDED FOR WRITING

Written expression is the final stage of literacy skill development. Difficulties experienced with listening, speaking, reading, and spelling can affect the ability to express thoughts in print or writing. There are many skills that successful writers need to use, such as the abilities to:

- initiate an activity;
- maintain attention to the task;
- type or write by hand;
- retrieve words;
- sequence words into sentences;
- use proper grammar, syntax, and punctuation;
- spell correctly; and
- organize the written content.

LOW-TECH ALTERNATIVES

To help children develop handwriting skills, a variety of positioning alternatives and low-tech options should be tried. Examples of low-tech options include alternative pens and pencils, pencil grips, slant boards, and special writing paper. There are also programs that have been developed, such as "Handwriting Without Tears" (http://www.hwtears.com), which may be used to teach legible writing. There is quite a bit of research on the development of writing skills in children. For more information, a great resource is LD Online (http://www.ldonline.org).

Two online sources for these low-tech options for improving written expression are:

- **Onion Mountain Technology** (http://www.onionmountaintech. com)
- **Therapro** (http://www.theraproducts.com)

CURSIVE

Cursive appears to be dying. When my teenage children were in elementary school, it was taught only during third grade. That was it. There is quite a bit of debate going on about this. Many students are now unable to read cursive writing. With the increase in technology use, more and more emphasis is being placed on keyboarding skills. However, there are many experts who believe that the learning cursive is important for brain development. Information on this topic can be found at Practical Parenting (http://www.practical-parent.com/home/2010/1/29/cursive-and-brain-science.html).

USE OF ASSISTIVE TECHNOLOGY WITH STUDENTS

If strategies and interventions to help the individual write well are not successful, it may then be time to consider assistive technology to help with written expression and the physical act of putting words onto the paper. There are many ways that mainstream and specialized assistive technologies can be used for students who struggle with the process of writing. Some AT tools help by providing another way to express thoughts and ideas to avoid the physical act of writing, while others help with particular aspects of written expression that may be especially difficult, such as word selection, spelling, grammar, and organization. There are also many technology tools that provide assistance by empowering students to improve skills for writing letters, words, sentences, paragraphs, and stories by offering engaging drill-and-practice stimuli with multisensory immediate feedback to facilitate learning. As mentioned often in this guide, it is imperative to evaluate the source of the writing difficulty and carefully select the appropriate technology tools.

FEATURES OF ASSISTIVE WRITING SUPPORTS

There are a number of mainstream features many technology products use that are helpful for struggling writers. Many students have difficulty writing essays by hand. It is often extremely helpful if they are encouraged or at least permitted to type responses to show what they know in school, rather than be held back by the process of writing by hand.

Text-based and picture-based word processors can greatly improve the quality of written work. The support provided with this type of software reduces physical effort and assists with organization so that writers are able to focus more on content. Mainstream word processors such as Microsoft Word and Apple's Pages software offer very helpful features that are beneficial for struggling writers. There are also specialized assistive writing technology products, apps, and features on browsers that offer a wide variety of helpful tools for people with dyslexia and dysgraphia. These tools can help students who have:

- illegible handwriting,
- very poor spelling skills,
- weakness or coordination problems which hinder writing by hand, and
- difficulty expressing thoughts in writing.

There are many students who are helped when they can have worksheets or tests made available to them on the computer or mobile device so that they can use assistive technology writing supports. Many students have poor handwriting and their legibility interferes with their production of written work. There are now apps that can take pictures or download worksheets and other PDF files into the app and enable the student to write on them. The newer mobile devices are preferred due to the improved cameras that are used for the scanning. Some can then resave the PDF and export it to a cloud-based product or the document can be attached to an e-mail.

Auditory feedback and text to speech. Auditory feedback and text to speech involve having the text said aloud after the user types a letter, word, sentence, or paragraph. When writers hear words or entire documents read aloud as they type, their written expression improves. The auditory feedback also helps writers maintain attention to their tasks, catch mistakes early to avoid lengthy editing sessions later, and may even improve word selection. Some products say the words aloud as the person types, while others permit the user to highlight words that were written and then read them aloud. This feature is now included on many computers, mobile devices, and browsers.

Autocorrect and abbreviation expansion. Autocorrect and abbreviation expansion both correct commonly misspelled words and allow users to input abbreviations to be expanded when typed. For instance, if the user types "IST," the program could be programmed to expand it and type "Innovative Speech Therapy." Users can create frequently used words, phrases, or other standard pieces of text, saving keystrokes and time.

Dictionary and thesaurus. Many dictionaries are now integrated into word processing programs and can be customized and allow grammar checks tailored to the user's needs. Some programs read selections aloud, while others offer assistance "thinking of words" to users with word retrieval challenges. There are some products made for people with very significant spelling and grammar challenges.

Editing. All word processing programs have methods of copying, cutting and pasting, and formatting the presentation of the document. Some programs, such as Microsoft Word and Apple's Pages, enable users to see the changes that others make to their documents with a feature called "Track Changes." The writer can decide whether to reject or accept the changes.

Multilanguage support. Some of the word processing programs are able to be used in multiple languages. There are apps and websites that translate text.

Online access and collaborative tools. There are now many online word processing programs that empower users to write online so that the content can be accessed from a variety of devices that are online, even if they use different operating systems. Examples of these programs are Google Docs and Microsoft Office web apps, which enable users to work "in the cloud." These tools generally are quite convenient because the user is not tied to one computer and can more easily share documents with others. Working online is ideal for writing documents, especially when a group of people need to make changes in a document or a person desires to access documents from multiple computers. Real-time coediting is available so more than one person can edit a document at the same time. It offers automatic file saving with easy access to earlier versions and it exports and imports most standard formats.

Organizing and outlining. More and more word processing systems assist with organizing written projects. Many of these programs offer the user the ability to work on an outline prior to writing the document. Some of the programs do so in a linear form; others use more of a brainstorming technique with webs. Each entry contains an idea, a concept, or a question that is visually linked together by branches to show they relate to each other. The user can have access to pictures, spell checkers, and text to speech. Brainstorming results can be converted into an outline and then edited to a finished product. It's also helpful to have the ability to organize ideas in outline mode and expand or collapse topics and drag and drop them where needed.

Picture or graphics support. Many individuals with communication and cognitive deficits are unable to read and write words. Pictures help improve written expression. Communication devices enable users to express themselves by clicking on pictures to generate written messages. Some software programs, quite a few mobile apps, and many dedicated communication devices on the market offer dynamic display. The user is initially presented with a set of pictures. Once an item is selected, more choices open up on the screen until the user finds the desired picture. Many of these items were discussed in Chapter 5: Augmentative and Alternative Communication.

Speech/voice recognition. With speech- or voice-recognition software, a user is able to speak and have the text written that they say. Some programs require more training and articulatory precision than others. This is now becoming a mainstream feature on many tablet computers. The image of a microphone can often be found on the keyboard. Sometimes, the more the system is used, the better able it is to understand what the user is saying. Incorrect words need to be corrected by either voice or keyboard commands in order to train the program for increased accuracy. Speech recognition provides potential hurdles for people with disabilities—especially those with intact cognitive and communication skills who have a visual or physical deficit that prevents them from being able to type well.

Spelling and grammar assistance. Different word processors offer diverse types of spelling and grammar guidance. Some are equipped to help typists who can produce phonetic approximations of words. Other programs tailor the type of grammar to be focused on during the grammar check.

Study skills assistance. Almost all word processing programs offer the ability to highlight text. Some also enable the user to extract the highlighted material and put it into a separate file for studying. Easy access to bookmarking, notetaking, summarizing, paraphrasing, and a dictionary are helpful study skill features of some word processors. By using the "find" feature, users can search for individual bookmarks and highlights. Text notes are helpful for visual processors, aiding the user to revisit and study important material. Using voice notes, users can dictate information such as oral summarizing and paraphrasing.

Visual presentation. Most word processing programs enable the user to change the background, text color, font, and size to promote increased comprehension and retention of material.

Web access with visual and auditory support. Several of the more advanced programs offer the ability to highlight, read aloud, and extract information from the web to other files.

Word bank. The word bank is often helpful for lists of topic-specific words to be presented to assist with the writing process.

Word prediction. Word prediction helps with many aspects of written literacy skills, such as word retrieval, spelling, and sentence formation. This type of software can improve the user's attention span, confidence, independence, and language development. It may minimize the number of keystrokes for those with physical difficulty typing. The use of grammatical word prediction has been shown to improve the sentence structure and grammatical accuracy of text. Programs vary in the prediction methods used. Many advanced word processing programs offer the user a list of words after a letter has been typed or selected, based on previous words used. Some provide word lists based on spelling and frequency of word usage in prior documents, and phonetic approximations of words that are written. Some programs enable the user to select the way the words are shown to the typist and the number of words to be included in the list. Keep in mind that in some instances word prediction programs may actually interfere with the writing process. The word list may be distracting and having to stop and choose words may slow down some writers.

SELECTION OF AN EFFECTIVE ASSISTIVE WRITING TECHNOLOGY

Word processing software and assistive writing products help with the speed and effectiveness of the writing process. They differ in the features included, the level of assistive support they provide, the way they are presented, and the cost. Some products include written materials for the educator as well as downloadable lessons with particular subject content that correlates with the school curriculum.

Begin by selecting the features that are most important for your particular situation and then try a few products with those features. Sometimes the more features that are available, the better the product; in other instances, the simpler the product, the better. Also, consider price, need to be online, the technology device it will be used with, and the availability of training and continued support for the product.

There are products that work within their own word processing systems and others that work in Microsoft Word or with other formats such as e-mail or the Internet. A few products are used more in the elementary and middle school years, because they offer supportive materials that are an integral part of school curriculum. Others are geared to higher level students and people in the working world.

SPECIALIZED ASSISTIVE TOOLS FOR SPELLING, GRAMMAR, AND WORD PREDICTION

MOBILE DEVICE APPS

Abilipad
by Cheryl Bregman
http://www.appytherapy.com/abilipad
- A customizable keyboard and adaptive notepad with word prediction and text to speech.
- iOS
- $19.99

Assistive Express
by Assistive Apps
http://www.assistiveapps.com
- This app offers word prediction, adjustable speed for speech output, and a favorites list for commonly used sentences.
- iOS
- $24.99

Clicker Docs
by Crick Software
http://www.cricksoft.com/us/products/apps/clicker-docs.aspx
- This app provides a child-friendly keyboard, word prediction, word banks, text to speech, and built-in Dropbox support. Curriculum support is provided through the many downloads available at Learning Grids.
- iOS
- $30.99

Co-writer

by Don Johnston, Inc.

https://itunes.apple.com/us/app/co-writer/id674099732?mt=8

- This app offers word prediction, spelling and grammar support, text to speech, and the ability to export documents.
- iOS
- $17.99

Grammar Checker

by Ginger Software Mobile

http://www.gingersoftware.com

- This app offers spelling and grammar support.
- Android
- Free

iWordQ US

by Quillsoft Ltd.

http://www.goqsoftware.com

- This app offers word prediction, speech feedback, abbreviation-expansion, and sharing of text online.
- iOS
- $24.99

Typ-O

by Second Guess

http://typ-o.com

- This app offers assistance using word prediction, spelling, and text to speech.
- iOS
- $4.99

ONLINE SUPPORTS

Ghotit's Online Spelling and Grammar Checking Service

http://www.ghotit.com

- Free

Ginger
by Ginger Software
http://www.gingersoftware.com
- This site offers a grammar checker, sentence rephraser, personal trainer with customized exercises, and text reader.
- Windows
- $89 for Premium version or $4.90 per month for basic

Read & Write for Google
by Text Help
- This is purchased from the Chrome web store (https://chrome.google.com).
- This web app can be used with PDF, ePub, and Google Doc files.
- Features include Read Aloud with dual color highlighting, Talking and Picture Dictionaries, Translator, Fact Finder, and Study Skills, as well as Annotation tools.
- Online in Chrome browser
- Free (additional purchase for premium features after 30 days)

WriteOnline
by Crick Software
http://www.cricksoft.com/us/products/apps/writeonline-app.aspx
- This app offers word prediction, natural-sounding voice output, Wordbar support, and many other curriculum supports.
- Mac and Windows
- $300

COMPUTER-BASED SUPPORTS

Real Writer & Reader
by Ghotit
http://www.ghotit.com/get_it_now
- Mac and Windows
- $29.99 a month or $194.95

WordQ + Speak Q

by Quillsoft

http://www.goqsoftware.com

- This app offers word prediction and text to speech on PC and Mac. It also offers a forgiving speech recognition option on the PC for people who are unable to use other speech recognition software due to slightly inarticulate speech patterns.
- There is also an iOS app called iWordQ for $24.99.
- WordQ + SpeakQ for PC is $279
- WordQ for Mac is $199 (Speak Q is not available for Mac)

Write Now

by Premier Literacy

http://www.readingmadeez.com/products/WriteNow.html

- This app offers text to speech, word prediction, word assist, confusables and homonym support, and writing analytics.
- Online and Windows
- $59.95

ANNOTATING OR TYPING ON PDFS (WORKSHEETS)

Many of these apps can be used to complete worksheets, help with notetaking when there are handouts, or help with taking tests. Some are able to be printed directly from the app, attached to an e-mail, or synced to a cloud service such as Dropbox, Google Drive or Evernote.

Goodreader

by Good.iWare ltd.

http://www.goodiware.com/goodreader.html

- iOS
- $4.99

iAnnotate

by Branchfire

http://www.branchfire.com/iannotate

- Android and iOS
- $9.99

PaperPort Notes
by Nuance
http://www.paperportnotes.com
- Allows for dictation
- iOS
- Free

Skitch
by Evernote
http://evernote.com/skitch
- Android and iOS
- Free with in-app purchases

Type on PDF
by Tipirneni Software
http://www.tipirnenisoftware.com
- iOS
- $4.99

APPS TO SCAN DOCUMENTS AND CONVERT TO PDF

There are many apps that are able to take a picture to create a PDF of text. Some also enable you to convert the document into an editable format or save as a PDF which is searchable. Internet access may or may not be needed for the OCR, depending on the app. Some offer searchable text.

Droid Scan Pro PDF
by Trans-code Design
http://droidscan.com
- Android
- $4.49

JotNot Scanner Pro
by MobiTech 3000 LLD
http://www.mobitech3000.com
- iOS
- $.99 (offers in-app purchases)

Mobile OCR Free
by Smart Mobile Software
http://www.smartmobilesoftware.com/mobile-ocr.html
- Android and iOS
- Free for Android; $2.99 for iOS

Scanner Pro
by Readdle
http://readdle.com
- iOS
- $6.99

SmartScan + OCR: Text Reader with PDF Conversion
by Andrew Sulimoff
http://www.amaximapps.com
- iOS
- $3.99

TEXT-BASED WORD PROCESSORS WITH SUPPORTIVE FEATURES FOR COMPUTERS

Google Docs
by Google
http://www.docs.google.com
- Google Docs offers cloud-based document editing and storage and real-time editing. It facilitates collaboration.
- Free

Kurzweil 3000
by Kurzweil Educational Systems
http://www.kurzweiledu.com
- This is a comprehensive reading, writing, and learning software solution including test-taking and study skill tools created for struggling writers with many helpful features.
- An app called Firefly is available for Kurzweil users so it can be accessed on tablets.
- Mac and PC
- $1,395

Launch Pad

by Premier Literacy

http://www.readingmadeez.com/products/LaunchPad.html

- This is a feature-rich package of assistive technology tools to help with reading and writing, online or offline.
- $399.95

Microsoft Word

by Microsoft Corporation

http://www.microsoft.com

- Word is now included in the MS Office 2013 and MS Office 365 web apps.
- Accessibility features can be found at http://www.microsoft.com/enable.
- There are many apps that permit users to use Word files on an iPad.
- Please refer to website for pricing options.

Pages

by Apple

http://www.apple.com/iwork/pages

- This is the word processing program included on most Apple computers.
- $19.99

Read & Write

by TextHelp

http://www.texthelp.com

- There is a Read & Write for the Desktop (PC and Mac) for $645; Read & Write for Google (when working online in the Chrome Browser; it's free); and Read & Write for iPad (iReadWrite, $19.99, and Reading Champion).

Real Writer & Reader

http://www.ghotit.com

- Mac and PC
- $29.99 per month

SOLO Literacy Suite

by Don Johnston

http://www.donjohnston.com/solo

- This is a full-featured writing solution with curriculum supports.

- It includes Co:Writer 6, Write: OutLoud, and Draft:Builder.
- Mac and PC
- $290, $84, and $125, respectively
- SOLO is $773

WriteOnline

by Crick Software

http://www.cricksoft.com

- This is an online full-featured product with word prediction, text to speech, graphic organizing tools, and Wordbars to support writing.
- It can be used online or offline if installed on a computer.
- It features settings for users with low vision and an on-screen keyboard for switch access and scanning.
- Compatible with Moodle learning platform.
- There is a WriteOnline app for iOS for $30.99. The WriteOnline app has a more mature look for middle school students and older when compared to the Clicker Docs App.
- Curriculum support with Learning Grid Resources.
- $300 for single user

WYNN

by Freedom Scientific

http://www.freedomscientific.com/LSG

- This full-featured word processing software uses four color-coded rotating toolbars. Users can highlight text directly on a web page and extract the text into a WYNN document.
- Includes electronic notecards and writing templates aligned with the Common Core State Standards.
- $375 or $995 with scanning (OCR) software

TAKING NOTES

There are quite a few good notetaking apps on the market. They are generally not as full featured as the word processing programs described earlier in this chapter, but are often very helpful for students. Most offer basic editing functions, some record as the person writes or types, a few are especially helpful for people with visual challenges, most can read aloud using features within the app or device, and many help with organizing notes for future reference. Additional helpful features include the ability to sync content to cloud-based services such as Dropbox, Evernote, and

Google Drive, tag files, and search for particular words. Some also enable the note taker to choose his or her desired size and type of font, set margins, and adjust contrast between the text and background as well as the screen brightness. Some are compatible with the dictation features and text-to-speech features of the mobile devices. Some allow both handwriting or typing, while others permit only one. There are also apps that will record as the user takes notes. This has been an area of enormous growth. Below are a few of my current top picks. Details are not included since they are changing so fast. Please refer to websites for more information.

· ·

Capture Notes 2
by G8R Software LLC
http://captureapps.com/capturenotes
- iOS
- $5.99

Nebulous Notes
by Nuclear Elements
http://nebulousapps.net
- iOS
- $3.99

Notability
by Ginger Labs
http://www.gingerlabs.com
- iOS
- $2.99

Notes Plus
by Viet Tran
http://notesplusapp.com
- iOS
- $8.99

Super Note
by Clear Sky Apps
http://www.clearskyapps.com/portfolio/supernote
- iOS
- $2.99

MyScript Notes Mobile
by Vision Objects
http://www.visionobjects.com/en/myscript/about-myscript
- Android, iOS, and Windows
- $7.99

Evernote
by Evernote
http://www.evernote.com
- Android, iOS, Mac, and Windows
- Free

PRESENTATIONS

It is becoming more accepted in school for students to be able to demonstrate knowledge using multimedia, rather than just written, reports. Here are a few tools that are very helpful.

Glogster
by Glogster Edu
http://edu.glogster.com
- Mac, Online, and Windows
- $10 for a 1-year subscription on the home version

Haiku Deck
by Haiku Deck Inc.
http://www.haikudeck.com
- iOS
- Free

Pictello
by AssistiveWare
http://www.assistiveware.com/product/pictello
- iOS
- $18.99

Powerpoint

by Microsoft

http://office.microsoft.com/en-us/powerpoint

- Mac and Windows
- $109.99

Prezi

http://prezi.com

- iPad, Mac, and Windows
- Free, upgrades available

SoftMaker Presentations Mobile

by Softmaker Software GMBH

http://www.softmaker.com/english

- Android
- $4.99

STORY CREATORS

Individuals who have difficulty with communication can create stories to assist with expression.

Bookabi

by Tamajii

http://tamajii.com/bookabi

- This app allows users to create stories, including background, characters, objects, stickers, or your own photos. Speech bubbles, text, and a cover can be added.
- iOS
- Free (with in-app purchases)

I Like Stories

by Grasshopperapps.com

http://www.grasshopperapps.com/i-like-stories

- Many books are included that can be customized. Students can add their voice and text to each page.
- iOS
- $.99

Story Patch
by Haywoodsoft, LLC
http://storypatch.com
- iOS
- $.99

Storybird
http://storybird.com
- Mac, Online, and Windows
- Free

Storybook Maker
by Merge Mobile
https://itunes.apple.com/us/app/storybook-maker/id593996170?mt=8
- iOS
- $3.99

Toontastic
by Launchpad Toys
http://launchpadtoys.com/toontastic
- iOS and Online
- Free

PICTURE-BASED, TALKING WORD PROCESSORS

People with severe reading and writing deficits who are unable to use text-based word processors to write are often able to benefit from picture-based, talking word processors. These programs typically offer speech feedback, symbols or pictures to support text, and on-screen grids for writing and communication. Users create written documents by either typing directly into the word processor or by clicking on-screen grids that contain symbols, words, or letters. These programs enable the therapist or parent to create writing activities specifically suited to individuals, incorporating as much or as little picture and sound support as needed.

Clicker

by Crick Software

http://www.cricksoft.com

- Students can write with words or pictures by selecting items in a customizable grid at the bottom of the screen.
- There is an extensive picture library with wizards for sentence building, word banks, writing books, matching, and language activities.
- Switch accessible
- Access to many resources on Learning Grids
- Mac and Windows
- $300 for a single computer license

Clicker Sentences

by Crick Software

http://www.cricksoft.com/us/products/apps/clicker-sentences.aspx

- Similar to Clicker, described above.
- iOS
- $26.99

Picture Word Power

by Nancy Inman

http://www.inmaninnovations.com

- This program is designed for augmentative communication.
- It can be purchased as an iOS app for TouchChat as well as several dedicated communication devices.
- $299.99

GRAPHIC ORGANIZERS: TECHNOLOGY FOR ORGANIZING WRITTEN NARRATIVE

For many people with writing challenges, one of the most difficult steps of the writing process is getting started. Brainstorming thoughts without regard to the order, spelling, or forming sentences can help. The use of visuals is very effective for struggling writers. Outlining and semantic webbing along with the use of images can help organize ideas, help students show what they know, and can assist with converting those visual maps into outlines. Some organizational tools need to be loaded onto a computer; others will work online or on a tablet. They vary greatly in features. In the business world the use of mind maps has become increasingly popular to keep track of information, present information, and create plans. Paper organizers have been used in the schools for many years. Digital supports are becoming increasingly popular.

There are mobile apps, online programs, and software for Mac and Windows computers that are helpful to writers who need assistance with developing ideas, organizing, outlining, and brainstorming. There are comprehensive literacy software programs described earlier such as Kurzweil 3000 by Kurzweil Education Systems and Read & Write by TextHelp that include many of these features. Users build graphic organizers by combining pictures, text, spoken words, video, and links to represent thoughts and information. Using images or graphs can help people with reading and writing challenges understand abstract concepts in a concrete way. Graphics combined with text can facilitate learning better than text alone. Software such as Inspiration allows users to input text or pictures in smaller segments and slowly build them into a finished document. Diagrams are easily converted to outlines. When finished writing, the user can convert the document into Microsoft Word or another format to export.

By using visual mapping/graphic organizers, writers are often more easily able to:

- sequence and expand writing,
- create study aids,
- organize projects,
- enhance critical thinking and comprehension of information,
- take notes,
- collaborate with others, and
- create presentations to show knowledge.

Here are some products that can be used to help with brainstorming and visual presentation of material:

- **bubbl.us** (https://www.bubbl.us), a free web app to brainstorm online
- **Kidspiration** by Inspiration Software (http://www.inspiration. com), a feature-filled product with excellent video tutorials and common core curriculum supports; Mac, Online, and Windows; $23.97
- **Webspiration** by Inspiration Software (http://www.inspiration. com); $6 per month
- **Inspiration** by Inspiration Software (http://www.inspiration.com), $39 for a single desktop computer download version
- **Inspiration Maps** by Inspiration Software (http://www.inspiration. com), can share files with the desktop version; iOS; $9.99

- **MINDOMO** by Expert Software Applications (http://www.mindomo.com), desktop and tablet versions and online tools that can be synced; eight export formats and six import formats; $6 per month

Additional Graphic Organizers can be found at these two very helpful sites:

- **UDL Tech Toolkit** (http://udltechtoolkit.wikispaces.com/Graphic+organizers)
- **Lauren Enders' Pinterest** (http://pinterest.com/lasenders/graphic-organizer-mind-mapping-apps/)

TECHNOLOGY TO HELP WITH THE PHYSICAL ASPECT OF WRITING AND TYPING

The physical act of writing is problematic for many people who have fine motor coordination problems and weakness in their upper extremities. Those with mild physical difficulties may benefit from the accessibility options included with many operating systems and browsers.

- **Apple Products:** http://www.apple.com/accessibility
- **Microsoft Products:** http://www.microsoft.com/enable
- **Google Products:** http://www.google.com/accessibility

ALTERNATIVE INPUT DEVICES

Writers with severe physical difficulties may benefit from alternative input devices. These may include, but are not limited to, adaptive keyboards, keyguards, switches, touch screens, head-operated and eye-gaze pointing devices, Morse code input devices, brain-actuated pointing devices, voice input systems, speech-to-text software, voice-recognition or voice-command software, and cursor enlargement software.

An on-screen keyboard displays a visual keyboard with all of the standard keys. You can select keys using the mouse or another pointing device, or you can use a single key or group of keys to cycle through the keys on the screen. There are many different designs of onscreen keyboards, each having their own specific features and functionality. Most devices now include on-screen keyboards.

ALTERNATIVES FOR MOBILE TOUCH SCREEN INPUT

Swype
http://www.swypeinc.com
- This is an input method for touch screens which uses one continuous finger or stylus motion connecting letters to input words faster.
- Android
- $.99

SlideIT
http://mobiletextinput.com
- To input text on a touch screen, the user slides a finger or stylus across letters and words appear. The person does not have to worry about being extremely accurate.
- This program uses word prediction and is available in many languages.
- Android
- $3.99

SPEECH TO TEXT/SPEECH RECOGNITION

It is incredible how much the world of speech recognition has changed in the past several years. It is now an included feature in most of the newer mobile devices to be able to say words aloud and have the tablet or phone type out what you said. This is often a huge help to struggling writers, but not a miracle cure.

The biggest advantage of the fully featured speech recognition software, such as Dragon NaturallySpeaking by Nuance (http://www.nuance.com/dragon/index.htm), was the ability to do hands-free computing, which still is very helpful for people with limited mobility or a disability with written expression. It used to be the case that using speech recognition programs required very clear speech, extensive training time, memorization of multiple commands, considerable practice, a substantial cognitive load, and quite a bit of money.

Speech recognition software until recently has been very difficult for people who have communication and cognitive deficits. It is still difficult, but new advances have opened doors for individuals who have mild communication and cognitive challenges. Mobile devices and new operating systems on computers and tablets are using technology that requires less training. It is also possible to combine the speaking with typing, which makes the process easier for many individuals. On many new devices, a microphone can be seen as part of the on-screen keyboard.

Even though this type of assistive technology has recently improved quite a bit, it is still not a magic cure for students who have writing challenges. In order to effectively use voice recognition, a person has to have the cognitive and language skills to organize the material that they want to say and then speak slowly and distinctly and organize the content in an effective manner. Most students find this difficult unless the material that is spoken is short or they have organized the content ahead of time using a combination of visual and text supports.

For a review of the mainstream products, please take a look at TopTenReviews (http://voice-recognition-software-review.toptenreviews.com).

Here are a few mobile apps and computer software products with speech recognition that are available:

- **Dragon Dictation Mobile Apps** by Nuance (http://www.nuance.com/dragonmobileapps) for most mobile devices
- **Dragon NaturallySpeaking** by Nuance (http://www.nuance.com/dragon/index.htm) for PC
- **Dragon Dictate** by Nuance (http://www.macspeech.com) for Macs
- **SpeakQ** by Quillsoft (http://www.goqsoftware.com). This is the product that I most often use when working on a Windows computer with an individual who has communication or cognitive challenges. It is an add-on to WordQ software and the total cost is $279.

ADDITIONAL TOOLS TO HELP WITH WRITTEN EXPRESSION

LiveScribe Pen
by LiveScribe
http://www.livescribe.com

- This pen records all that is said as the user writes. The recorded audio can be replayed by tapping directly on the special dot paper with the pen that recorded the audio.
- The recorded notes and audio when using the Sky Wifi version are sent automatically to a personalized Evernote account that includes 500MB of storage space.

- Videos (pencasts) are available through Evernote and searchable on any computer or most mobile devices via free apps.
- MyScript from Livescribe provides handwriting recognition so that the text can be converted to a Word document.
- Creative users can use this pen to create talking flash cards, schedules, communication boards, and memory books by recording speech on the special paper and then cutting up the paper and putting it on index cards or in a scrapbook.
- 2 GB Sky Wifi Smartpen holds 200 hours of recorded audio.
- $149.95

CHAPTER 10

DRILL-AND-PRACTICE TECHNOLOGY TO
IMPROVE WRITING SKILLS

There are quite a few programs patterned in a drill-and-practice format to improve writing skills. It is important to practice both typing and writing by hand, which are both valuable skills. To simulate writing with a pencil, a stylus can be used. If there is a keyboard it is usually best if it is a QWERTY keyboard rather than in ABC order.

There are hundreds of products available to use for improving written expression. I did my best to represent here a wide selection of products that I have used the most often and, in my opinion, are a good value. For pricing information I generally included a full-featured product for home use with one individual. There may be free versions or more fully featured versions for school use.

Many great products are not included in this guide. There are just too many. What one person finds disappointing may be a goldmine for another person with different needs. Hopefully those that I included will help you get started in your search for the most appropriate drill-and-practice tools to improve written expression. I have included products from a variety of vendors for a variety of devices and levels. I also included products that offer one or more of the following:

- engaging activities and/or graphics,
- excellent value for a limited budget,
- ability to become easier or harder based on user performance,
- ability to be used on multiple types of devices,
- customizability,

- track progress,
- evidence basis,
- alignment with common core curriculum, and
- unique features.

Here is a list of what I believe to be the top five developers (in alphabetical order) that offer effective programs to improve written expression. I have used multiple products from these companies for many years:

- **Crick Software** (http://www.cricksoft.com): This company has developed a wide variety of softwares, online tools, and apps to support struggling readers and writers.
- **Don Johnston** (http://www.donjohnston.com): This company has been around for more than 32 years and offers assistive technology tools that are used in more than 32,000 schools to help students with a wide variety of learning challenges.
- **Inspiration Software** (http://www.inspiration.com): This company offers products that assist with using visual tools along with many unique features to enhance writing.
- **Merit Software** (http://www.meritsoftware.com): I have used Merit's products for many years. They offer a wide variety of programs to help students in third through 12th grade improve reading comprehension, vocabulary, writing, and grammar. Some tools are available to download onto a computer and others can be used online.
- **Mobile Education Store** (http://mobile-educationstore.com): This company produces a wide variety of iOS apps to support language and literacy for students of all ages. I communicated with the developer (Kyle Tomson) and was quite impressed as I learned about his newest endeavors—creating interactive, engaging iTextbooks with many embedded supports for literacy, which look wonderful. He is also in the process of developing apps for Android devices.

WRITING LETTERS OF THE ALPHABET

123s ABCs Handwriting Fun
by TeachersParadise.com
http://www.teachersparadise.com

- Android
- Free

iWriteWords
by gdiplus
http://giggle-lab.com/iwritewords
- iOS
- $2.99

LetterSchool
by Boreaal
http://letterschool.com
- iOS
- $2.99

Touch and Write
by Fizzbrain LLC
http://fizzbrain.com
- Several versions available
- iOS
- $2.99

Write My Name
by NCSoft
http://www.injini.net/?page_id=2108
- iOS
- $3.99

Writing Wizard
by L'escapadou
http://lescapadou.com
- iOS
- $2.99

WRITING WORDS/SPELLING

The signs or symptoms of spelling problems may include, but are not limited to, the following examples:
- reversals and confusion of letters like b and d,
- omission of letters (called elisions),
- use of letters or syllables in the wrong order, and
- spelling words phonetically (how they sound).

Learning to spell correctly is a difficult task to master. If reading issues are present, the same underlying deficits that contribute to difficulty in reading also contribute to challenges with spelling. It is especially difficult when certain skills are weak, such as:

- analyzing and recognizing the whole as being made up of individual parts,
- perceiving letter sounds and remembering them,
- decoding written words, and
- remembering sequences.

Many helpful suggestions for improving spelling can be found at LD Online (http://www.ldonline.org/article/5587; http://www.ldonline.org/article/6192). There are many products developed primarily for spelling help. A quick search with the word "spelling" on Amazon or in an app store will reveal a host of resources. In addition to mainstream products, there are also a few specialized programs created for people who may need to use switches or keyboards. Some of the programs that provide help with spelling during writing tasks will generate a list of misspelled words which then can be used in spelling lists to study. There is also now a rapidly expanding number of spelling apps available. A review of all of them is beyond the scope of this book. To explore the world of spelling apps, type in the word "spelling" when searching in the online store and explore all that is available.

Alphabet, Spelling and Phonics!
by Tribal Nova
http://www.ilearnwith.com
- iOS
- Free

BigIQkids Spelling Program
by BigIQkids
http://www.bigiqkids.com
- iOS and Online
- Free

Chicktionary for iPad
by Blockdot Inc.
http://chicktionarycoop.com
- iOS
- Free

Crossword Adventure for Kids
by Rob Ellis
http://zellissoftware.com
- iOS
- $1.99

Droid Spell Kids
by VG Web Solutions
http://www.vgwebsolutions.com
- Android
- Free

First Words Deluxe
by Learning Touch
http://www.learningtouch.com/products.htm
- iOS
- $4.99

Freefall Spelling
by Merge Mobile
http://mergemobile.com
- iOS
- $1.99

Montessori Crosswords
by L'Escapadou
http://lescapadou.com
- Android, iOS, and Mac
- $2.99

Rocket Speller
by Little Big Thinkers
http://littlebigthinkers.com
- iOS
- Free

Simplex Spelling

by Pyxwise Software

http://www.pyxwise.com/simplexspelling.html

- A series of apps that has received numerous awards and is especially helpful for students who don't respond to other spelling methods
- iOS
- $4.99

Skill Builder Spelling

by Ben Kaiser

http://kaiserapps.com/spelling

- iOS
- Free

SpellingCity

by SpellingCity

http://www.spellingcity.com/vocabularyspellingcity-app.html

- Android and iOS
- Free

Cimo Spelling (Sight Words) and Cimo Can Spell (Sound Out Words)

by PlaySmart-Kids

http://playsmart-kids.appspot.com

- iOS
- $2.99

Squeebles Spelling Test

by KeyStageFun

http://www.keystagefun.co.uk/squeebles-spelling.html

- Android and iOS
- $1.99 for iOS and $2.49 for Android

DRILL AND PRACTICE APPS FOR WRITING SENTENCES

Editor in Chief Software

by Critical Thinking Co.

http://www.criticalthinking.com

- Series of software

- Mac and Windows
- $14.99

First Phrases

by Hamaguchi apps

http://hamaguchiapps.com/First_Phrases_App.html

- iOS
- $15.99

Grammar Fitness Online

by Merit Software

http://www.meritsoftware.com

- Multiple levels
- Mac, Online, and Windows
- $39 a year for one user for one year

Grammar Jammers

by Pearson Education

http://support.pearsonschool.com

- Series of three apps
- iOS
- $2.99

GrammarPrep

by Pearson Education

http://www.pearsonhighered.com/grammarprep

- Series of apps
- Android and iOS
- $3.99

Jumbled Sentences

by Innovative Net Learning Limited

http://www.inlearning.hk

- Series of apps
- iOS
- Free

No-Glamour Grammar Interactive Software

by Carolyn LoGuidice

http://www.linguisystems.com/products/product/display?itemid=10345

- Mac and Windows
- $43.95

Punctuation Puzzler Software
by Critical Thinking Co.
http://www.criticalthinking.com
- Mac and Windows
- $4.99

SentenceBuilder
by Mobile Education Store
http://mobile-educationstore.com/apps/sentence-structure-apps/sentence-builder
- iOS
- $5.99

Sentence Builder App
by Abitalk Inc.
http://www.abitalk.com
- iOS
- $4.99

Sentence Maker
by GrasshopperApps.com
https://www.itunes.apple.com/us/app/sentence-maker/id499150658?mt=8
- iOS
- $.99

Sentence Workout
by Virtual Speech Center
http://www.virtualspeechcenter.com/Resources/sentence_workout_app.aspx
- iOS
- $12.99

WRITING PARAGRAPHS AND STORIES

How to Write a Paragraph
by Classroom Complete Press Ltd.
http://classroomcompletepress.com
- iOS
- Free, in-app purchases

First Author Writing Software

by Don Johnston

http://donjohnston.com/firstauthorsoftware

- Takes students through the process of choosing a topic, selecting a prompt, and writing with built-in supports
- $179

Paragraph Punch Online

by Merit Software

http://www.meritsoftware.com/software/starter_paragraph_punch_online

- Interactive online paragraph writing tutorial
- Mac, Online, and Windows
- $29

TYPING

There are many software programs that assist with typing. A comprehensive review of the many types of products available is beyond the scope of this guide. There are also a few free online programs. A few websites that review typing software are:

- http://www.superkids.com/aweb/pages/reviews/typing
- http://typing-software-review.toptenreviews.com

Here are a few programs that I have used the most in my practice:

Custom Typing Training

by Custom Solutions

http://www.typingtraining.com

- Mac, Online, and Windows
- $9 per month, individual subscription

Dance Mat Typing

by BBC Schools

http://www.bbc.co.uk/typing

- An interactive typing tutorial that contains animated typing tutors
- Free

Type to Learn 4: Agents of Information
by Sunburst
http://ttl4.sunburst.com
- Mac and Windows
- $39.95 for home version

CHAPTER 11

TECHNOLOGY AND STRATEGIES TO
IMPROVE EXECUTIVE FUNCTION AND NEW LEARNING

THE NATURE OF COGNITIVE IMPAIRMENTS

Cognitive impairments in planning, organization, memory, reasoning, attention, learning, judgment, and self-awareness are prominent road-blocks for learning and independence. Impaired cognition can be detrimental to education efforts. The level of deficits can be severe or subtle. Students with impaired executive functioning or cognition may display the following characteristics:

- reduced attention and difficulty concentrating during a task,
- inability to sequence and organize information,
- poor analytical skills and judgment,
- difficulty figuring out solutions to problems,
- a hard time learning and retaining new information,
- inefficient time management skills,
- slow processing of new information,
- deficit planning and initiating goal-oriented behaviors,
- lack of motivation,
- limited ability to initiate activities,
- impulsive behaviors, and
- faulty awareness and denial of deficit areas.

We are all constantly bombarded by new information. In our fast-paced society, it's often difficult to keep up with the many demands in our lives, even at a young age. Students who experience these challenges may encounter the following problems:

- forgetting homework or assignments,
- tuning out what is said in class,
- procrastinating necessary tasks,
- becoming distracted or easily overwhelmed,
- losing items,
- being scattered or cluttered,
- appearing lazy,
- experiencing difficulty learning new information,
- showing trouble following through with planned activities,
- experiencing issues with prioritizing daily activities, and
- being disorganized at home or school.

Detailed information on the causes of executive function, learning, memory, and cognitive deficits and potential medically based treatments is beyond the scope of this book. However, the following websites provide helpful information on how executive functioning, memory, and cognition work; types of diagnoses and symptoms; treatment, prevention, and screening; alternative therapy; specific conditions; related issues; clinical trials; and research:

- **Children and Adults with Attention Deficit/Hyperactivity Disorders** (CHADD; http://www.chadd.org)
- **LD Online.org** (http://www.ldonline.org)
- **National Center for Learning Disabilities** (http://www.ncld.org)
- **National Institutes of Health** (http://www.nlm.nih.gov/medlineplus/memory.html)
- **National Institute of Mental Health** (http://www.nimh.nih.gov)
- **National Institute of Neurological Disorders and Stroke** (http://www.ninds.nih.gov)
- **Smart Kids With LD** (http://www.smartkidswithld.org)

TREATMENT APPROACHES

As with communication issues, it is important to first differentially diagnose the aspects of cognition to sort out relative strengths and weaknesses. Factors that might adversely influence a student's abilities from one day to the next need to be limited. Negative contributors to impaired cognitive function may include lack of interest, sleep problems, stress, a noisy environment, and other external distractions. For many individuals, a neuropsychological evaluation, in which memory, problem solving, visual-spatial skills, language skills, and executive functioning skills are tested, is helpful. The tests are comprehensive and will more clearly describe cognitive skills, both weak and strong.

STRATEGIES TO ENHANCE LEARNING

When teaching students new information, no matter what the age or content, there are certain guidelines that are helpful for everyone. For individuals with more difficulty learning, they are even more critical to use to help speed along the learning process. Teachers, therapists, and parents should make efforts to:

- make sure there is attention to the task or change the task to gain interest;
- increase active engagement using multiple senses;
- provide lots of repetition and embedded redundancy;
- offer visual support;
- use content that is of high interest and interactive;
- help the student relate to what he or she already knows;
- use multisensory teaching tools—the more hands-on the learning approach, the better;
- encourage students to learn from each other and collaborate;
- practice retrieving the information to be learned;
- spread out study sessions—don't cram;
- stay organized; and
- limit distractions whenever possible.

I stress that when I help students improve cognitive skills it is necessary to move along two paths simultaneously. I work to improve weak skills while compensating for them. The compensatory strategies may be something that the individuals do on their own, or something that is done by another person or device to change the environment or task to promote success with the activity. It is critical to know your student and to tailor input and output methods to enhance success. In addition, the use of state-of-the-art technology as well as strategies that do not involve technology are often needed.

IMPROVING COGNITIVE SKILLS

The first part of cognitive retraining—improving specific skills—typically includes exercises to improve attention, concentration, memory, organization, perception, judgment, and problem-solving skills. Treatment most often uses a drill-and-practice method with increasingly challenging tasks. Cognitive abilities are expected to improve, much like a muscle gets stronger with increased exercise. Stimuli gradually increase in difficulty.

A criticism of this method is that the cognitive training exercises are essentially artificial and have little relevance to real-world functional cognitive challenges. However, quite a bit of research supports the notion that appropriate practice techniques can help improve memory, learning, and cognition. The premise is that new neurological pathways are formed, and improved performance enhances cognitive abilities when clients are confronted with real-world challenges. Many of the products that employ this drill-and-practice approach include research study reports on their websites. Examples include:

- **Lumosity.com** (http://hcp.lumosity.com/research)
- **Positscience.com** (http://www.positscience.com/why-brainhq/world-class-science)

COMPENSATORY APPROACH

The second component of cognitive training is learning to use strategies, compensatory techniques, and tools to cope with weaker areas. Learning to use these tools not only compensates for impaired ability, but also may help build the skill itself. The compensatory approach to improving memory and cognition generally focuses on the functional activities that take place both at home and at school.

Assistive technology tools can help a student plan his or her schedule, stay organized, and keep track of his or her responsibilities. There are a wide variety of tools that can assist with becoming more independent and successful with memory and cognitively challenging tasks. Calendars, schedules, task lists, contact information, timers, alarms, the Livescribe Sky Wifi Pen, mobile devices, cell phones, online resources, and computers can help clients manage, store, and retrieve information as well as improve time management, memory, and new learning. Prior to turning to technology-based solutions, it may be helpful to work on tasks such as:

- establishing routines;
- organizing and reducing clutter;
- minimizing distractions and stress;
- establishing a supportive environment;
- engaging in cognitively challenging activities;
- breaking down seemingly overwhelming tasks into manageable pieces in order of priority and doing them one at a time;

- using calendars to improve time management, organization, and memory; and
- using timers and alarms to help users remember to take medication, leave for a class, or track time during a task.

GENERAL GUIDELINES AND THOUGHTS TO ENHANCE LEARNING

Everyone benefits from routines throughout the day, such as in the morning to prepare for school, and establishing a sequence of activities that routinely take place once a student returns home from school.

Establish concrete goals with clear expectations that are reasonable and achievable.

Incorporate the use of checklists and calendars into daily activities, especially for problem spots such as mornings, evening rituals, and homework.

Technology can be a wonderful tool, but it's *how* solutions are implemented that matters most. Many affordable cutting-edge technologies can supplement and create new ways of learning. These tools benefit everyone, not just students with special needs. First take a look at what the student already has and is comfortable using.

Many mobile technologies (phones, tablets, etc.) and computers include helpful built-in features and native apps which are included when you purchase the item, such as:

- the ability to dictate reminders using speech recognition and read directions aloud using text to speech;
- clock apps with alarms and timers (the iPad has a visual timer);
- maps with ability to "pin" locations to help remember where things are located; and
- calendar apps to organize the day, week, and semester.

Before purchasing additional products, watch online videos by going to the website of the technology or search on YouTube for videos about how to use the many features of the device. Many families as well as professionals are often not aware of the features of items they already have.

TIME MANAGEMENT TOOLS

There are many technologies available to help individuals become more organized and efficient. There is no one "correct" time management or organizational system. However, if not properly set up, too many systems or a system that is too complicated can make things more difficult. Calendars are the most important tool for improving executive functioning.

Thoughts about paper calendar systems:

- Many students already use a paper assignment book for school. It may be preferable over digital systems for school assignments if supports are provided and working and using digital systems will force the student to enter information twice.
- Paper calendars are better than no calendar at all.
- For individuals who are reluctant to switch to a digital solutions, ask the following questions: What happens if the paper calendar/book is lost? Does the student need to spend time rewriting information? Do frequent changes cause the written material to be illegible? Would it be helpful to be able to share the information with others who don't have access to the assignment book?

Considerations for establishing systems for time management:

- Students need to be taught how to effectively use calendars, not to just be handed the technology or paper product. When I start with a student I review the reasons why the calendar is important, the type of information that should be added, and when to use it—which is different for each person.
- It may take time to initially set up a calendar and time management system, but will end up saving time in the long run.
- Take time to learn what time management systems are already in place in the family, with friends, and at school.
- Students who are old enough should play an active role in selecting their calendar.
- There needs to be a way to easily refer to contacts, calendar, and to-do lists.
- Easy access with a backup is critical. Digital systems can be backed up online and accessed from different devices or copied periodically to a hard drive. Paper-based systems need to have a phone number to call and "reward if found" information in a visible spot in case of loss.
- Avoid clutter and lots of little notes and reminders scattered in different places.
- Keep calendars for home and school lives in one place.
- Start children at a young age using calendars. At first, calendars with visual supports are the most appropriate. Gradually add the use of text as they learn to read.

- When students are old enough to actively help manage their schedules, they need to keep the system with them for quick reference as needed, especially as they become responsible for adding items to their schedule. Mobile devices are great for quickly accessing phone numbers, calendar information, and for reminder systems.
- When reviewing time and task management apps, many appear to be free, but then in-app purchases are needed to sync information between devices or access the data online.

SELECTION OF TECHNOLOGIES TO SUPPORT TIME MANAGEMENT

There are many online calendars and apps for all types of mobile devices that can help manage time and schedules. Most of them have the following helpful features:
- multiple display/viewing options such as the current day, week, or month;
- color coding options;
- ability to easily schedule recurring events and edit events; and
- reminders and alarms.

An idea that has been reiterated throughout this book is the importance of making a good match between needed and offered features of technologies. In addition to the above features, there are calendar and organizational apps that do the following:
- sync information between different devices;
- search data for a particular person, location, or word;
- offer sharing capabilities so that others can view and input information;
- present information in picture form for people who can't read;
- integrate tasks and to-do lists or checklists into the calendar and assign due dates;
- help keep track of school schedules, teachers, assignments, and grades;
- provide reminders and alarms that can be sent by text, e-mail, beeps/chimes, or vibration;
- enable users to attach pictures and maps to notes and appointments;
- add and share multiple calendars with varying levels of permision for the users;
- support time, period and block scheduling in schools;
- track classes, assignments, and tests;

- offer teachers the ability to enter assignments, the syllabus, and other information and have the student sync the information directly into their calendar without copying it;
- organize assignments by due date, course, or priority;
- be available in multiple languages;
- offer video tutorials to help get started;
- access content and add information whether online or offline;
- tag items to later view as a group;
- offer reminders based on the user's location; and
- estimate time for an activity to help with planning.

Below is a sampling of available resources. There are hundreds. I have selected the items I feel have one or more of the following qualities:

- are the best value,
- can be used on multiple platforms,
- offer a unique features, or
- are especially helpful for students with special needs.

Please be sure to search online for the newest products available. More products become available daily!

. . . .

Checkmark
by Snowman
http://www.builtbysnowman.com/checkmark

- This is a location based reminder and to-do app.
- iOS
- $9.99

Evernote
by Evernote Corporation
http://www.evernote.com

- Evernote.com enables users to keep to-do lists, schedules, or any type of note, web clip, or photo. Photos and notes are searchable using tags, which are multiple key words that can be used to search for an item.
- Android, iOS, Mac, and Windows
- Free

First Then Visual Schedule
by Good Karma Applications
http://www.goodkarmaapplications.com/first-then-visual-schedule.html
- For children of all ages who have communication and cognitive challenges as well as difficulty with transitions, this visual app helps lower anxiety and increase independence.
- iOS
- $9.99

Google Calendar
by Google
http://www.calendar.google.com
- This is a very popular multifeatured online calendar that can be synced to most devices. It is usually what I start out using with most of my clients. I then set it up to sync with other apps on devices. The interface is similar to desktop calendar applications such as Microsoft Outlook and iCal and their calendar files can be imported. The young student's calendar is typically shared with parents.
- Android, iOS, Mac, Online, and Windows

iPrompts® Pro
by Handhold Adaptive, LLC
http://www.handholdadaptive.com
- This includes the features of many standalone apps in one. It includes a visual schedule app, timers, choices and visual countdown timer, the ability to create or customize social stories, and real-time feedback on speech loudness, rate, and stress.
- The user has the ability to print or e-mail the schedule, choices, or stories by e-mailing as a PDF or printing them. Voice can be recorded to accompany each of these programs.
- More than 30 video modeling clips are included to show proper school and social behavior. A voice chart provides feedback on speech loudness and "voicematch" provides feedback on rate, stress, and speech rhythms.
- These three programs can be purchased separately as iPrompts ($50), StoryMaker ($40), and SpeechPrompts ($20).
- iOS
- $99.99

iStudiez Pro

by Kachalo and Balashoff

http://www.istudiez.com

- This is a fully featured app created for high school and college students or parents helping younger children stay organized. There is another app called iTeacherBook which can sync assignments into the student's calendar in addition to other features that will help manage students.
- iOS and Mac
- $2.99

MyHomework Student Planner

by Rodrigo Neri

http://www.Myhomeworkapp.com

- Students add classes or other activities, enter classes using time, period, and block scheduling and schedule reminders. If the teacher uses Teachers.io and sets it up, info such as the syllabus, attachments and resources, and announcements will automatically be synced.
- This app is appropriate for middle school age and older.
- Android, iOS, Online, and Windows
- Free

Now What

by Richard Humphrey

https://itunes.apple.com/us/app/now-what/id434244026?mt=8

- This is a simplified task/schedule app that was developed for children who need help with knowing what comes next and making transitions to new activities. Adding and deleting features are password protected.
- iOS
- Free

Picture Planner

by Cognitopia Software

http://www.cognitopia.com

- This is an iOS app that is free and that will allow the information that has been purchased for a computer to be viewed on a mobile iOS device. This picture-based personal organizer functions as a calendar for individuals who are unable to read or have cognitive challenges.

- Individuals can create customized picture-based daily schedules for school, self-care, or chores. Users can upload their own pictures or use photos, which are included. The schedule uses pictures, text, and text to speech and can be printed or exported to other devices. It offers an easy way to input recurring activities, pop-up reminders, and a simple user interface.
- Mac and Windows, iOS app if you purchase the computer version
- $199

Remember the Milk

by Remember the Milk

http://www.rememberthemilk.com

- This is an online to-do list and task management tool that integrates well with mobile and web apps. Offers multiple organization methods for lists, including tags and time estimates. See tasks based on location. Uses multiple reminder messages.
- Android, Google apps, iOS, Mac, Online, and Windows
- Free

Spoty Location Reminder

by Incorporate Apps

http://www.incorporateapps.com

- This is a location-based reminder, location alert, call blocker, and profile changer.
- Android
- $1.49

Tasks N Todos Pro

by Handy Apps

http://www.tasksntodos.com

- This is a to-do list that syncs automatically with Google Tasks and offers due dates, notes, and reminders.
- Android
- $5.99

Todoist

by Doist

http://en.todoist.com

- This project management app separates lists into projects and then tasks and subtasks. The user can drag and drop tasks to reorder and check off items when done and leave or archive. Deadlines can be set and labels color-coded.

- Android, iOS, Mac, Online, and Windows
- Free

Visual Schedule Planner

by Good Karma Applications

http://www.goodkarmaapplications.com/visual-schedule-planner1.html

- This customizable, visually appealing calendar for the iPad integrates pictures, video, and voice output. Events that require support can be linked to a video or activity schedule for task modeling. Timers, reminders, notes, and checklists can be added.
- iOS
- $14.99

Watchminder Watch

by Watchminder

http://www.watchminder.com

- This is a programmable vibrating reminder watch that looks like a standard sports wristwatch, but the watch vibrates and a reminder message discreetly appears.
- The watch has 30 daily alarms and a person's entire day can be pre-programmed, with alarms activated at specific times of the day and messages/reminders displayed.
- Older students find the watch helpful for time management and pacing during exams.
- $69

The following products are also helpful.

2Do Tasks Done in Style

by Guided Ways Technologies Ltd

http://www.2doapp.com

- Android and iOS
- $9.99 on iOS and $6.99 on Android

Awesome Note (+ ToDo)

by Bridworks

http://www.bridworks.com

- iOS
- $3.99

Calendars+
by Readdle
http://readdle.com/products/calendars/
- iOS
- Free

CalenMob-Google Calendar Client
by Blue Tags
http://www.appxy.com
- iOS
- Free or $6.99 for Pro version

Schedule Planner
by Intersog
http://intersog.com/portfolio/schedule-planner-pro
- Android and iOS
- Free or $8.99 for pro version

Simple Student
by Michael Spade
https://www.facebook.com/SpadeApps
- iOS
- Free

Errands To-Do List
by Yoctoville
http://www.yoctoville.com/errands-app-details
- iOS
- Free

APPS TO VISUALLY SUPPORT AND PROMPT SEQUENCING STEPS IN A TASK

Many students have significant difficulty sequencing tasks during the day, transitioning to new activities and making choices. Learning is greatly enhanced and stress reduced when they are offered engaging visual supports to provide prompts for understanding upcoming events, making choices, and focusing on the task at hand.

Many features may be offered in these apps, including:
- templates for daily activities;

- step-by-step multimedia instructions to perform a task;
- choice-making supports;
- countdown timers;
- the ability to add customized audio, text, pictures, and video;
- the ability to add multiple users;
- locking features;
- many stock photos; and
- supportive video tutorials to teach how to use the app.

The following are very helpful apps for students in need of this type of support.

iPrompts®
by Handhold Adaptive
http://www.handholdadaptive.com
- Android and iOS
- $49.99

See-quence . . . My Schedules at School
by I Get It
http://igetitapps.com/applications/i-see-quence-series/i-see-quence-my-day-at-school
- One in a series of apps
- iOS
- $4.99

Choice Board Creator
by Techno Chipmunk
http://technochipmunk.blogspot.com
- iOS
- Free

Visual Impact Pro
by AbleLink Technologies
http://ablelinktech.com/index.php?id=130
- iOS
- $49.99

TOOLS TO HELP WITH STUDYING AND ONLINE ORGANIZATION

Technology tools can greatly enhance an individual's ability to learn new information. Often, a combination of traditional studying approaches and innovative cutting-edge resources creates a more motivating environment for the learner. Online flash cards, software that provides assistance with reading, writing, and organization, an app that can be used as an interactive Whiteboard to record writing and sound, and a pen that can record audio, when used creatively, can empower learners to become more successful. These tools allow students to take advantage of learning strengths and to help compensate for learning weaknesses. Many of these products are also highlighted in other sections of this book.

FLASH CARD PROGRAMS

There are a variety of mobile apps and web-based programs that allow users to create and use flash cards for online study or studying with a mobile device. Most require the user to set up an account, which is often free of charge. Digital flash cards are a great way to learn concrete information such as English vocabulary words, foreign languages, or calculation problems. It's not necessarily an appropriate way to learn more complex interrelated information. Many can either be private or shared with others. Students can pool their resources and share flash cards created for studying, or a tutor, teacher, or therapist can create them. It is usually possible to import pictures and/or audio, and many use "tags," which are keywords to group the content in different ways. Multiple languages are supported in quite a few of them and most offer a system to help study missed items.

Digital flash card apps and online sites can be used to:

- access millions of premade flash card sets or make your own;
- work with flash cards that have two–five sides;
- use images with camera to create flash cards;
- listen to cards using built-in text to speech or record your own audio;
- create cards using Excel, or online storage systems such as Dropbox or Google Drive;
- track progress;
- keep track of the cards you know;
- filter decks to search by specific cards, previously erred, or topic;
- share decks with others;
- organize decks in folders and combine them;

- study while online or offline; or
- print flash cards.

These are a few sources of online premade decks and quite a few apps are now available to help access and interact with those sources. They include:

- **Quizlet** (http:www.quizlet.com)
- **Cram** (http://www.cram.com)
- **Course Hero** (http://www.coursehero.com)
- **Study Stack** (http://www.studystack.com)

The following are some apps that can be very effective to use for learning new information.

- -

Flashcards+

by Connor Zwick

http://flashcardspl.us

- This app can filter decks to search for particular cards, select which cards in a deck to study, and autoplay audio for cards.
- It supports many languages and is compatible with Quizlet and Course Hero.
- Free or $1.99 for voice output and $2.99 for "flashcloud" to sync decks across devices and share with friends

Flashcards++

by Jason Lustig

http://www.iphoneflashcards.com

- Download and sync apps from Quizlet and Cram, advanced "spaced repetition algorithm," sync flash cards, and study data between devices.
- iOS
- Free

Flashcard Machine

by Flashcard Machine Mobile, LLC

http://www.flashcardmachine.com

- This app allows users to tag cards based on location.
- Android and iOS
- Free

gFlash+ Flashcards & Tests
by gWhiz LLC

http://www.youtube.com/watch?v=H1ZK0-8y5GE
- This app is integrated with Google Drive, Quizlet, and StudyStack. Decks can be purchased from Kaplan, Barron's, and other professional sites. This app offers the ability to use images, sound, and a multiple choice question format.
- Android and iOS
- Free or in-app purchase options for no ads and professional flash cards to use.

Quizlet
by Quizlet, LLC

http://quizlet.com/mobile
- The app is very basic. Users cannot edit with it on an iDevice.
- Many families think that if you use the Quizlet online flash cards, you have to use this app, but many others offer many more features.
- Android and iOS
- Free

INTERACTIVE WHITEBOARD APPS

Whiteboard interactive apps can be used to help students with homework or to teach a lesson and make it available for future reference in person or online. These apps resemble recordable whiteboards that are often used in the schools. There are several available which may provide the following abilities:
- create video tutorials,
- record voice,
- upload photos,
- draw pictures or type,
- use multiple colors,
- share online, and
- replay content in any web browser (that supports Flash) or from an iPad.

Helpful apps include:

. . . .

Doceri
by SP Controls
http://www.doceri.com
- iOS
- Free with in-app purchases

Educreations Interactive Whiteboard
by Educreations
http://www.educreations.com
- iOS and Online
- Free for basic functioning

Explain Everything
by MorrisCooke
http://www.explaineverything.com/about.html
- iOS
- $2.99

Lensoo Create
by Lensoo Inc.
http://www.lensoo.com
- Android
- Free

ShowMe Interactive Whiteboard
by Learnbat
http://www.showme.com
- iOS
- Free

Splashtop Whiteboard
by Splashtop
http://www.splashtop.com/whiteboard
- Android and iOS
- $19.99

SOCIAL AND VISUAL BOOKMARKING TOOLS FOR ONLINE CONTENT

The Internet is playing an increasingly important role in the way we obtain and organize new information. It used to be that people would print website pages onto paper and highlight and file them or type the URLs for future reference. There are now many tools that are extremely helpful with online information management. Internet users can share, organize, and search for information using social bookmarking tools. Users save links to webpages and can make them public or private, or specify e-mail addresses that can view them. The system can rank a resource based on the number of viewers who have bookmarked the site using different tags. I use Diigo (http://www.diigo.com) and Evernote (http://www.evernote.com) all the time in my speech therapy practice and for personal use to remember products, websites, and ideas found online. I want to be able to quickly locate the sites I have found in the past as well as network with others to learn about sites they have found helpful.

. . . .

Diigo
http://www.diigo.com
- This allows users to highlight in multiple colors and add sticky notes to webpages, archive websites and pages, and make them searchable by tags or full text. Users can also organize items by tags or lists of URLs. Information can be private or shared with others. To see what others have tagged that may be of interest, try searching words such as "assistive technology," "special education apps," and "dyslexia."
- Android, iOS, Mac, Online, and PC
- Free for basic needs

LiveBinders
http://www.livebinders.com
- LiveBinders is another free online tool to collect resources and organize them. It can be public or private and thought of as a three-ring notebook. The resource links are located along the top of the page. Multiple "binders" can be placed on shelves to assist with organization.
- Certain features are only available for paid subscribers.

Symbaloo

http://www.symbaloo.com

- Symbaloo is a free online tool that can be used to simplify the process of accessing favorite sites for individuals who have difficulty with the process. It is essentially a free customizable start page for websites.
- Click on an image and the user is taken to the page. The user can drag and drop items to organize them. If he or she touches or clicks on one of the tiles, the embedded link takes him or her to the site. The items can be searched and users can view their home "webmix" or browse the collections of others.
- SymbalooEdu is an educational version of this product that was created to share favorite websites with students. Once educators, parents, or therapists have made a grid of tiles which are actually URL links, they can be shared with others via e-mail. This can be a very helpful tool for young students or students with intellectual impairments.

SOFTWARE WITH EMBEDDED STUDY TOOLS

Quite a few of the assistive technology tools that were reviewed earlier in this book to help with reading and writing are very helpful for learning new information. Products with text-to-speech capabilities can improve new learning due to the increased retention of written information when it is simultaneously read aloud and highlighted by a computer. Brainstorming software and other tools to help users learn new information presented graphically can be quite effective. Products that record as the user writes are extremely useful for helping students review and remember information that was taught. The ability to mark up printed info by writing on PDF files when studying is also very helpful.

Almost all word processing programs offer the ability to highlight text. Some also enable the user to extract the highlighted material into a separate file for studying. Easy access to bookmarking, notetaking, summarizing, paraphrasing, and a dictionary are helpful study skill features of some word processors. Text notes are helpful for visual processors, aiding the user to revisit and study important material. Using voice notes, users can dictate information such as oral summarizing and paraphrasing.

Below are some software products that can be used to improve study skills. All of the products offer text to speech and word prediction, but some also offer the ability to:

- summarize written material;
- bookmark a location in a document;
- add voice notes, sticky notes, footnotes, or text notes into a document;
- use notes that the user can have read aloud when double clicked; and
- extract highlighted key points from a document then transfer them into another document to use as a study aid or for a research project.

Many have been described in previous chapters. Please refer to websites for more information. Some of them have apps available, but sometimes the apps are not as fully featured as the versions that are Windows or Mac-based.

- **Inspiration** by Inspiration Software (http://www.inspiration.com)
- **Kurzweil 3000** by Kurzweil Educational Systems (http://www.kurzweiledu.com)
- **LiveScribe Pen** by LiveScribe (http://www.livescribe.com)
- **Microsoft Word** by Microsoft Corporation (http://www.microsoft.com)
- **Read and Write Gold** by Text Help (http://www.texthelp.com)
- **Read:OutLoud** by Don Johnston (http://www.donjohnston.com)
- **Talking Word Processor** by Premier Literacy (http://www.readingmadeeasy.com)
- **Wynn Scan and Read Literacy Software** by Freedom Scientific (http://www.freedomscientific.com)

TOOLS THAT RECORD AS YOU WRITE

There are a myriad of affordable options now available that link written notes with audio. This is very helpful for many students with special needs. There is a pen, mainstream software, and mobile device apps that offer this ability to simultaneously record what is said aloud as people write. It is very powerful when a student can take notes, select a certain place on a page, and play the audio aloud to hear what was said when the text was written or a picture was drawn. Everything you type, handwrite, or draw while recording is synced. The recordings can be saved online and shared with others. This is especially helpful for students:

- with attention challenges who miss content that is spoken;
- who have difficulty multitasking and are unable to process information and learn as they write;

- with memory issues and slow processing who benefit from repetition of information;
- who miss class and benefit from hearing what was said as well as reading another person's notes; and
- who need to learn how to take better notes.

Some apps offer a wide variety of features and others focus on just one or two features. It's important to decide which features are most important in your situation. Sometimes using one app to meet a variety of needs is appropriate, and at other times, keeping things simpler is better. Features of these products may include the following:

- a variety of drawing tools with different colors;
- advanced word processing features such as text boxes, outlining, and bullets;
- a zoom window for handwriting with a palm rest;
- use of photos;
- the ability to annotate on top of PDF files for students who are given class outlines;
- organizational tools to help manage classes, homework, and exam dates;
- variable speed playback; and
- the ability to auto sync and share files with others via cloud services such as Dropbox, Google Drive, or Evernote.

Sky Wifi Livescribe Pen
http://www.livescribe.com

- In addition to empowering students to use a real pen and paper (which are produced as part of this product), the latest pen automatically sends the recorded notes wirelessly to an Evernote account that is free for up to 500 MB of storage.
- Using Evernote, users can quickly search and share the notes with users on most tablets, phones, and computers.

MOBILE DEVICE APPS

A range of features are offered with these note-taking apps that will record as you write.

. . . .

AudioNote
by Luminant Software Inc.
http://luminantsoftware.com/iphone/audionote.html
- Android, iOS, Mac, and Windows
- $4.99

Complete Class Organizer
by AnimalBrainz
http://www.completeclassorganizer.com
- iOS
- $4.99

Notability
by Ginger Labs
http://www.gingerlabs.com
- iOS
- $2.99

SoundNote
by David Estes
http://soundnote.com
- iOS and Mac
- $4.99

Microsoft Office
by Microsoft
http://office.microsoft.com/en-us/onenote-help/record-audio-and-
video-notes-HA010121254.aspx
- Features Audio Notes toolbar that allows users to record audio into
  the document through a built-in or external microphone.
- Prices may vary depending on the package.

While Audio Note can record using Word 2004/2008 for Mac,
Microsoft Word for Windows 2007 or earlier will not take Audio Notes.
In Word for Mac, if you take written notes as you record audio, playback
will display an arrow next to the point in your notes that you were writing
at that time. The Audio Notes can be exported. The following are potential
uses for these recording and notetaking tools:

- **Individual notetaking accommodation:** A student with an auditory processing problem, impaired hearing, attention deficit dis-

order, or dysgraphia may take few or unclear notes. Rather than relying on a scribe in class, the student may independently access the information when needed using these tools.

- **Entire classroom use:** Assign a different student to take notes each day and share the notes online with all students in a classroom. If someone was absent or is having trouble learning information, that person can view the video online and see the text that was written while hearing the teacher. All students can hear their teacher's explanation over and over as long as they have online access.

Syncing recorded audio to written notes is one of the best assistive technology tools available for many students, but complications may arise over legalities and concerns regarding recording other students in the class. In many, if not all places, it is the law that you have to get permission from a person prior to recording him or her. Also, I have met resistance in some schools that will not allow students to use any recording device in the classroom. They state that there is presumed confidentiality in school and they don't want the other children recorded. Be sure to investigate the legalities in your setting prior to using these recording devices. Student do need to be careful not to distract others with these tools. If they need to listen to content during class, they should be instructed to wear headphones.

ONLINE COLLABORATION

There are now many technology tools that allow individuals who are far apart to collaborate online, which can be very effective when studying or completing a group project. Screen sharing or desktop sharing can be used so that an individual enables another person to view his or her desktop or screen from a distance and view videos, software, or documents. In some cases, the person can hand over the ability to control the desktop to the person viewing from a distance. Sometimes it is first necessary to download a small free program. Free desktop sharing and meetings can take place at the following websites:

- **Google+** (http://www.google.com)
- **Facebook** (http://www.facebook.com)
- **Skype** (http://www.skype.com)
- **Join.me** (https://join.me)
- **Anymeeting** (http://www.anymeeting.com)

Online collaborative workspaces allow groups of people to work together on common documents in various formats either synchronously (at the same time) or asynchronously (at different times). Documents can be public or private. Online workspaces include the following:

- **Google Drive** (http://www.docs.google.com)
- **Titan Pad** (http://www.titanpad.com)
- **Pirate Pad** (http://www.piratepad.net)
- **Sync.in** (http://sync.in)

Videoconferencing/video chat allows two or more locations to interact via two-way video and audio transmissions simultaneously. People can see each other while speaking. Features may include the ability to:

- see each other and speak at the same time,
- show others photos and documents,
- schedule sessions in advance, or
- video chat with up to 10 people at a time for free.

Google Hangout
http://www.google.com

- This has become very popular with students.
- Users need to have a free Google+ account.
- E-mail correspondence can be upgraded to chat and then to a hangout by clicking on a photo in the chat list.

Skype
http://www.skype.com

- Voice and video calls as well as messages to anyone else on Skype are free.
- Conference calls with three or more people are available for a fee.
- Instant messaging, file transfer, and screen sharing are available.

ooVoo
http://www.oovoo.com

- Users can have free video chats with up to 12 people at a time.
- Users can use text chat and send files.

USE OF IMAGES TO SUPPORT LEARNING

Visual images help all people learn and function more productively in life, especially when used to assist people with cognitive challenges. Many of us have mobile devices with built-in cameras and computers and tablets with the ability to capture the image on the screen, but don't think to use it as an assistive technology tool to support individuals with cognitive impairments.

It is very easy to take screenshots on computers. This screen capture is often found on computer keyboards in the upper right corner as PRINT SCREEN (or PRTSC or PRTSCN). To capture the image on a screen, try pressing the function key (fn) at the same time as the Print Screen key to activate it, and the image is saved on the clipboard. To learn more about your particular computer and how to print the screen, go to the Help menu. Once you select the screen capture, you can paste it into Paint or another drawing program to resize, rotate, and crop it. Text can also be added. It can be very helpful to cut and paste screen shots into practice assignments to show people exactly what you want them to do on the computer.

Built-in still and video cameras have become commonplace on new devices and the quality keeps improving. It is now easier to share these images with others and save them for use in apps and communication devices. Sound, text, and special effects can be added to create ideal learning and communication tools.

In addition to using the still and video cameras, it is easy to take a picture of the screen on a mobile device. To do so on an iOS device, hold down the home and power button at the same time. On an Android device using the Ice Cream Sandwich or Jelly Bean (Android 4.x) operating system, you press the Volume Down and Power buttons at the same time. You should hear the sound a camera makes and see a bright light as a picture is taken. The picture of the screen is saved where you find your other pictures.

There are quite a few very inexpensive scanning apps which were reviewed in Chapter 7: Technology and Strategies to Improve Reading Comprehension, such as Scanner Pro by Readdle and JotNot Scanner Pro by MobiTech 3000. The images are very clear and saved as a PDF file rather than a JPEG file. The following are some ideas for using images:

- Take still or video pictures of daily activities to enhance communication and learning.
- Take pictures of items needed for school to avoid forgetting items.
- Take pictures of written homework assignments to avoid errors with copying the directions.
- Take still and video images of sign language and gestures a person uses to promote consistency among service providers and family with the prompting of signs for communication.
- Take pictures while out shopping for items, including pictures of price tags, to communicate the information to others.

- Take a picture of directions offered by a map app so that you can refer to it and not use data or run out of battery on your mobile device. There's no need to print out the turn by turn directions; they will just be with all the other pictures.
- Use Facetime, Skype, or another app that lets you see people as you speak to them so that you can point the camera to the image to share with others in real time. It's great whenever modeling an action is needed.
- Provide a series of screen shots to remind someone how to do something on a computer or tablet.
- Customize apps for more personal and engaging practice. Examples of apps which are better when they include pictures to teach cognitive and communication skills include AAC apps such as Proloquo2go by AssistiveWare (http://www.assistiveware.com/product/proloquo2go); Touchchat Suite by Silver Kite (http://www.silver-kite.com/touchChat); and Autismate by SpecialNeedsWare (http://autismate.com/Home/Comprehensive-App-For-Autism-With-Visual-Supports/).
- Early learning apps for auditory comprehension, vocabulary development, and literacy may also permit the user to upload images for practice, such as Word SLapPsVocabulary app by Zorten (http://zorten.com/slapps/wordslapps) and Little Matchups by Grasshopperapps.com (http://www.grasshopperapps.com/apps/little-matchups).
- Some apps incorporate talking and pictures, such as Pictello by AssistiveWare (http://www.assistiveware.com/product/pictello) and Tapikeo by Jean-Eudes Lepelletier (http://www.tapikeo.com/index_en.html).

LEARNING BY WATCHING VIDEOS

Many resources are available to enhance learning. Some require payment and others are free. Students understand best when visuals are used. The following are some helpful online resources to explore. All of these websites will work on Mac and Windows computers. Some will work online with all mobile devices and others will require free apps to function.

Academic Earth
http://academicearth.org
- This app features online courses from top universities and a series of thought-provoking videos.
- Free

Annenberg Learner

http://www.learner.org

- A wide selection of multimedia resources is available on this app for the professional development of teachers.
- Free

Big Think

http://bigthink.com

- Free videos of thought leaders in a range of fields are featured.

Brainpop

http://www.brainpop.com

- This is a paid subscription website with some free content.
- Animated videos are used to engage students in a wide variety of subjects aligned to state education standards.
- $99 per year

brightstorm

http://www.brightstorm.com

- This website offers 3,000 videos to help students with homework on a wide range of subjects by entertaining expert teachers.
- $9.99 a month for least expensive option

Cosmeo

http://www.cosmeo.com

- This subscription-based website uses video segments to aid visual learning and games.
- Many in-depth lessons and tutorials are included.
- $9.95 per month

Hippocampus.org

http://www.hippocampus.org

- This website offers education resources for students in high school and older.
- Free

iTunes

http://www.apple.com/itunes

- Teachers can upload content to iTunesU.
- Free

Khan Academy
http://www.khanacademy.org
- This website hosts a library of more than 3,500 lessons on a variety of topics.
- Free

MathTV
http://www.mathtv.com
- Math videos are available on a wide range of topics.
- Free

Neok12
http://www.neok12.com
- This website offers free educational videos, lessons, and games for students in K–12.

TeacherTube
http://www.teachertube.com
- A website similar to YouTube but with safe content for students. Includes a wide range of searchable videos.
- Free

TED
http://www.ted.com
- This website offers videos by top leaders and thinkers.

Watchknowlearn.org
http://www.watchknowlearn.org
- This website offers well-organized educational videos for K–12. Many are searchable by grade and Common Core Standards.
- Free

CHAPTER 12

INTERACTIVE PROGRAMS TO
IMPROVE COGNITION, LEARNING, AND MEMORY

FEATURES OF INTERACTIVE PROGRAMS

There are many computer software programs and mobile device apps on the market to improve cognitive functioning. They present engaging interactive opportunities accompanied with drill-and-practice exercises to improve attention, memory, perception, sorting, sequencing, categorization, reasoning, and other cognitive skills. They are helpful for children who experience attention and learning difficulties as well as people with autism and impaired intellectual functioning. Many programs have already been discussed in previous chapters. There are hundreds of products that could be included in this chapter. I have included the products in this section that:

- I tend to use the most in my therapy sessions with good results,
- automatically adjust the level of difficulty,
- track performance,
- can be customized to meet individual criteria,
- offer a unique set of features,
- are well priced,
- help a wide variety of students,
- can be used on multiple operating systems, or
- represent a variety of vendors that produce high-quality products to improve cognition.

INTERACTIVE PROGRAMS FOR IMPROVING COGNITION ON PCS AND MACS

BrainTrain Memory Gym PE
http://www.braintrain.com
- This program is for professionals to use with students. It offers more than 400 structured games using a video game reward system to improve attention, working memory, problem solving, and mental processing.
- PC
- Contact company for pricing for professional version.
- For home use of the Memory Gym program, the cost is $59 for one of the following: BrainTrain Memory Games (Primary Editions)- Memory Magic: designed for ages 6-8, or Memory Discovery: designed for ages 9-12.

Building Thinking Skills
by Critical Thinking Company
http://www.criticalthinking.com
- Mac and PC
- $29.99

HearBuilder Sequencing
by Super Duper Publications
http://hearbuilder.com
- $69.95 for home edition

Mindspring Software
by Marbles the Brain Store
http://www.marblesthebrainstore.com/mindspring-software
- Mac and PC
- $99.95

Mind Benders
by Critical Thinking Company
http://www.criticalthinking.com
- This is one in a series.
- Mac and PC
- Prices vary within the series.

ONLINE PROGRAMS TO IMPROVE MEMORY AND COGNITION

Be sure to also check out the resources provided in Chapter 13: Interactive Websites and Games to Promote Communication, Literacy, and Learning.

. . . .

BrainHQ
by PositScience
http://www.brainhq.positscience.com
- $14 per month

Lumosity.com
by Lumos Labs
http://www.lumosity.com
- $14.95 per month for full access

Brain Boosters
by Discovery Education
http://school.discoveryeducation.com/brainboosters
- Free

MOBILE APPS TO IMPROVE MEMORY AND COGNITION

Apps to improve memory and cognition are being added every day. Sometimes the best apps were not created to be used the way that I use them to help reach therapy goals and sometimes they are. It depends on what is motivating to the student and what the therapeutic or educational need is that is being addressed. Many apps can be used in different ways to work on a wide variety of goals. There are quite a few that, when used to improve cognitive skills, make the user feel that they are just "playing games." They can be effectively used during treatment sessions and as part of independent practice programs to bring a bit of fun into the learning process. Playing games can reduce stress, help participants enjoy acquiring new skills, and help individuals with communication and cognitive challenges find new ways to interact with others.

In addition to the drill-and-practice apps that work on cognitive retraining, I encourage the students I am helping to play carefully selected games on mobile devices (and the traditional type) during our time together and when interacting with family members and friends. When others are not available, most of the apps listed below can be played independently. Games can be rich in creating opportunities to practice communication and cognitive skills. As is true with all teaching and intervention efforts, they may need to be changed and adapted in ways to meet the needs of the student and to work toward established goals. This can be accomplished by exploring and selecting options that are provided in the game, changing what the student is expected to do, or by varying the amount of assistance provided during the game. Here are some to try. Some apps are listed in more than one category. As with other app lists, this is just a small percentage of apps available. I tend to prefer apps that:

- offer hints,
- show progress,
- enable a person to play alone or with another person,
- offer different levels of difficulty, and
- are easy to use.

The following apps are for working on higher level cognitive retraining.

Fit Brains Trainer
by Vivity Labs App
http://www.fitbrains.com
- iOS and Online
- $5 for 3 months; some apps are free

Charge Your Brain, HD
by Unusual Things
http://www.uthings.com/ibrain_world.html
- iOS
- Free with in-app purchases

Lumosity Mobile
by Lumos Labs Inc.
http://www.lumosity.com
- Android and iOS
- In-app purchase of one-year access to all of the activities is $79.99

The following apps are for working on moderate level cognitive tasks.

. . . .

4 in a Row Online
by Clever Fox
http://www.cleverfoxsoftware.com
- iOS
- Free

84 Logic Games
by Andrea Sabbatini
http://www.andreasabbatini.com
- iOS
- Free

ABA—Which Does Not Belong?
by Kindergarten.com
http://www.kindergarten.com
- One in a series
- iOS
- Free

Animal Hide & Seek Adventure
by Awesome Giant
http://animalhideandseek.com
- iOS
- $.99

Auditory Workout
by Virtual Speech Center
http://www.virtualspeechcenter.com/Resources/auditory_workout_app.aspx
- iOS
- $19.99

Basic Sequencing Skills
by Nth Fusion LLC
http://apps.nthfusion.com
- iOS
- $.99

Bejeweled
by Electronic Arts
http://www.popcap.com/games/bejeweled/home
- Bejewed Blitz, iOS Free
- Bejeweled 2, Android $2.99

Boggle
by Electronic Arts
http://www.ea.com/boggle-ipad
- Android and iOS
- $.99

Caboose Express: Patterns and Sorting
by @Reks
http://www.atreks.com
- iOS
- Free with in-app purchases

Categories Learning Center
by Smarty Ears
http://smartyearsapps.com/service/categories-learning-center
- iOS
- $9.99

Category Carousel
by Synapse Apps
http://pocketslp.com/our-apps/category-carousel
- iOS
- $6.99

Category TherAppy
by Tactus Therapy Solutions
http://tactustherapy.com/apps/category
- iOS
- $14.99

Charge Your Brain, HD
by Unusual Things
http://www.uthings.com/ibrain_world.html
- iOS
- Free with in-app purchases

Checkers Free
by Optime Software
http://www.optimesoftware.com/products/ipad/checkers_free
- iOS
- Free

Child Development Game Suite
by Injini
http://www.injini.net/?page_id=18
- iOS
- $29.99

Clean Up: Category Sorting
by Different Roads to Learning
http://www.difflearn.com/Apps
- iOS
- $1.99

Cookie Doodle
by Shoe the Goose
http://www.shoethegoose.com/CookieDoodle.aspx
- iOS
- $.99

Cut the Rope
by Zeptolab
http://chillingo.com/games/cut-rope
- Android and iOS
- Free

Doodle Buddy
by Pinger
http://www.pinger.com/content/home.html
- iOS
- Free

Dots- Online
by Clever Fox
http://www.cleverfoxsoftware.com
- iOS
- Free

EasyConcepts

by Easy Speak Enterprises

http://www.easyspeakenterprises.com/apps

- iOS
- $4.99

Find the Differences

by Pine Cone Software

http://www.androidgame365.com/puzzle/5331-find-the-differences-ii-game.html

- Android
- Free

Fun With Directions

by Hamaguchi

http://hamaguchiapps.com

- iOS
- $15.99

Guess the Code

by Optime Software

http://www.optimesoftware.com

- Android and iOS
- Free

Guess the Person?

by Richard Buckingham

http://itunes.apple.com/us/app/guess-the-person-hd-free/id515909521?mt=8

- iOS
- Free

isequences

by Fundación Planeta Imaginario

http://www.planetaimaginario.org/apps-ipad.html

- Option to translate the website into English
- Android and iOS
- $2.99

iSpotPro for Kids TE
by Mayuir Sidhpara
http://www.appycrumble.com/appycrumble/app-ispotpro-kids.html
- iOS
- $1.99

iTurnStones
by Intent Software
http://litegames.de/#home
- iOS
- Free

Jigsaw Box
by Sparkle Apps
http://sparkleapps.com
- iOS
- Free

Jigsaw Puzzles
by Intuitive Innovations
http://jigsawpuzzlesdeluxe.com
- iOS
- $1.99

Kids Memory Games
by Foundation Mir
http://www.amazon.com/Foundation-Mir-Kids-Memory-Games/dp/B007SP1W20
- Android
- Free

Kids Puzzles
by Grasshopperapps.com
http://www.grasshopperapps.com
- iOS
- Free

Kids Puzzles Puzzingo
by 77Sparx Studio, Inc.
http://www.77sparx.com/puzzingo
- Android and iOS
- Free with in-app purchases

Little Solver

by Innovative Mobile Apps

http://www.alligatorapps.com

- Preschool logic game
- iOS
- $.99

Logic Puzzles

by Puzzle Baron

http://www.puzzlebaron.com/portfolio-item/logic-puzzles

- Android and iOS
- $2.99

LogiGrid Logic Problem Puzzles

by Harmony Applications

http://www.harmonyapplications.com/LogiGrid.html

- iOS
- $1.99

Making Sequences

by Zorten Software

http://zorten.com/making-sequences

- iOS
- $4.99

MatchUp: Exercise Your Memory

by Magma Mobile

http://m.magmamobile.com

- Android
- Free

MatrixMatch 1

by MyFirstApp

http://www.myfirstapp.com

- iOS
- Free, in-app purchases are available

MemoryBlock

by Category 5 Games

http://category5games.com

- Android and iOS
- Free

Memory Matches 2

by IDC

http://itunes.apple.com/us/app/memory-matches-2/id500028364?mt=8

- iOS
- Free

Memory Train

by Piikea St. LLC

http://www.piikeastreet.com/apps/memory-train

- iOS
- $1.99

Memory Trainer

by Urbian

http://www.urbian.biz/apps/memorytrainer

- Android
- Free

MeMoves

by Thinking Moves

http://www.thinkingmoves.com/memovesapp.html

- Part of a more comprehensive program developed to help calm and focus children with autism and related disorders with the help of music and movement.
- iOS
- $9.99

Moofy Recognizing Pattern Games

by PlaySmart-Kids

http://playsmart-kids.appspot.com

- Android and iOS
- $1.99

More Buffet!

by Maverick Software

http://www.mavericksw.com/More_Buffet%21.html

- iOS
- $1.99

Music Sparkles

by Kids Game Club

http://kidsgamesclubhouse.com

- iOS
- Free

My Baby Gets Organized

by Baby Bus

http://www.baby-bus.com

- Android
- Free

My PlayHome

by Shimon Young

http://www.myplayhomeapp.com

- Android and iOS
- $3.99

My Zoo Animals: Toddler's Seek & Find

by Wonderkind Interaktionsmedien GmbH

http://apps.wonderkind.de/drupal/en

- iOS
- $1.99

One Step Two Step

by Synapse Apps

http://pocketslp.com/our-apps/one-step-two-step

- iOS
- $9.99

Pandora Radio

by Pandora Media

http://www.pandora.com

- Android and iOS
- Free

Pre-Number Category Sorting Matching Game
by Good Neighbor Press
http://www.goodneighborpress.com/apps.html
- One in a series
- iOS
- $.99

Preschool EduKidsRoom
by Cubic Frog Apps
http://www.cubicfrogapps.com/cubicfrogapps/edukidsroom
- One in a series of apps
- iOS
- $2.99

Sequencing Tasks: Life Skills
by Judy Lynn Software
http://www.judylynn.com
- One in a series
- iOS and Windows
- $7.99

Set Pro HD
by Set Enterprises
http://www.setgame.com/apps
- iOS
- $4.99

Solitaire
by MobilityWare
http://www.mobilityware.com/phoneApps/solitaire.php
- Android and iOS
- Free

Sort It Out
by MyFirstApp
http://www.myfirstapp.com
- One in a series
- iOS
- Free with in-app purchase

Sort This Out Pack
by Therapy Box Limited
http://www.tboxapps.com
- iOS
- $13.99

Spaced Retrieval
by Tactus Therapy
http://tactustherapy.com/apps/srt
- iOS
- $3.99

Speech With Milo: Sequencing
by Doonan Speech Therapy
http://www.speechwithmilo.com
- iOS
- $2.99

Splingo's Language Universe
by the Speech and Language Store
http://www.speechandlanguagestore.com
- iOS
- $2.99

Spot the Differences
by Weikuan Zhou
https://www.facebook.com/pagesCronlyGames/246908508659748
- iOS
- Free

Simply Find It Pro
by Simply Game
http://www.simplygame.net
- iOS
- $3.99

Spot the Differences
by Mad Rabbit
http://madrabbitstudio.blogspot.com
- Android
- Free

+Sudoku
by Mind the Frog
http://www.mindthefrog.com/en/sudoku/
- iOS
- $.99

Things That Go Together
by Grasshopperapps.com
https://itunes.apple.com/us/app/things-that-go-togethe/id490647359?
mt=8
- One in a series
- iOS
- $.99

Tic Tac Toe
by Optime Software
http://www.optimesoftware.com/products/ipad/tic_tac_toe_free/
- iOS
- Free

Toca Kitchen
by Toca Boca
http://tocaboca.com
- iOS
- $2.99

Toddler Puzzle Woozzle
by Swan Soft
http://www.woozzlegames.com/
- Android and iOS
- Free

Tozzle
by Nodeflexion.com
http://www.nodeflexion.com/iphone
- iOS
- $1.99

VAST Songs
by SpeakinMotion
http://www.speakinmotion.com/solutions/mobile-apps/vast-songs-series
- iOS
- $14.99

Visual Attention TherAppy
by Tactus Therapy Solutions
http://tactustherapy.com/apps/vat
- Provides systematic visual scanning and cancellation tasks
- iOS
- $9.99

Wheels on the Bus
by Duck Duck Moose
http://www.duckduckmoose.com/educational-iphone-itouch-apps-for-kids/wheels-on-the-bus
- iOS
- $2.99

CAUSE AND EFFECT APPS FOR STUDENTS WITH SEVERE COGNITIVE DEFICITS

There are many individuals with severe cognitive deficits who need help learning that their responses can cause something to happen. These individuals may display the following characteristics:
- no functional pointing response,
- no reliable gesture,
- unreliable yes/no response, and
- do not appear to pay attention to structured activities.

Families and educators typically have a hard time finding external sources of motivation. Some of these students have been diagnosed with severe autism spectrum disorder while others are labeled with profound intellectual disability. Assistive technology tools, such as cause and effect apps listed in this section using a touch screen on a tablet, can be very engaging and can be used to help create joint attention, environmental awareness, and focus for these students, which is often where therapy needs to start. Suggestions:

- **Generate interest.** I have found it helpful to first try to pique the individual's curiosity about the device before directly asking the student to do anything with it. Many people with severe deficits have never seen or touched a touch screen tablet. After observing the child and speaking to his or her teachers and family to get a sense of interests and capabilities, it is helpful to start by sitting beside the individual and using some of the cause and effect apps. This action typically generates interest from others in the room and I encourage others to try using the apps on my device. They touch the screen and see something happen. Sometimes this helps the individual become interested and they are more willing to try to interact with the apps. However, some students may find this interaction with others in the classroom enivornment to be overstimulating and it may be better to work in a distraction-free environment without others in the room.
- **Figure out the best selection method.** Once the person starts paying attention to the apps, help them use the appropriate gestures—touching, tapping, swiping, or producing sound. Observe the motion that seems easiest for the person. Some can touch and release well, while others are better at sliding their finger. If the child is unable to isolate a finger, it may help to put a glove on a student with the pointer finger cut out so that the tablet would only respond to the touch of that part of the finger.
- **Prevent the individual from exiting the app.** If you are using an iPad, use the guided access mode (which is available with iOS 6 and can be used on an iPad 2 or later) so that the student does not prematurely exit the app. Barbara Fernandes of Smarty Ears Apps is a speech pathologist and avid app developer who published a short video about using guided access. To view, go to http://www.geekslp.com/2012/09/geekslp-tv-33-how-to-use-and-set-up-guided-access-on-iOS-6-0.

Here are some of the thoughts I have in mind as I select apps:
- **Access:** What type of movement do I want to try? Am I going for a large movement or interaction where they can touch the screen anywhere, or do I want isolated single-finger control, which may be needed for an AAC app? Does the app require a tapping or sliding motion? Am I trying to elicit verbal sounds?
- **Motivating response:** What kind of response is motivating for this individual? Some apps have calm music while others offer exciting

music. Some apps have very busy, exciting visuals while others use simple, easy-to-see visuals.

- **Content:** What is appropriate content to match the individual's age?

Below is a list of apps that I have successfully used for developing interaction and joint attention. Repeated exposure may be needed to achieve results. Most of these apps I chose have movement, are highly visual, and provide sound or music to engage their users.

Balloon Bang
by Shiny Learning
http://www.shinylearning.co.uk/apps/index.shtml
- Android
- $1.49

Big Bang Patterns
by Inclusive Technology
http://www.inclusive.co.uk/apps/big-bang-patterns
- One in a series of apps, activities designed for use with children with low vision
- iOS
- $13.99

Bla Bla Bla
by Lorenzo Bravi
http://www.lorenzobravi.com/projects/bla-bla-bla
- Android and iOS
- Free

Cause and Effect Sensory Light Box
by Cognable
http://www.cognable.com/lightbox/
- Android and iOS
- $2.99

Color Dots
by Ellie's Games
http://elliesgames.com/color-dots
- One in a series of apps

- Android and iOS
- $2.99

Finger Paint with Sounds

by Inclusive Technology

http://www.inclusive.co.uk/apps/finger-paint

- One in a series of apps
- iOS
- Free

iLoveFireworks

by Fireworks Games

https://sites.google.com/a/fireworksgames.net/ilovefireworkslite

- iOS
- $.99

Injini Child Development Suite

by NC Soft

http://www.injini.net/?page_id=18

- iOS
- $29.99

Kaleidoscope Drawing Pad

by Bejoy Mobile

http://itunes.aple.com/us/app/kaleidoscope-drawing-pad/id52590407
0?mt=8

- Android, Blackberry, iOS
- Free

Knee Bouncers Great Play With Purpose

by KneeBouncers

http://www.kneebouncers.com/

- Extremely interactive basic early literacy activities, a series of apps
- Android and iOS
- Free with in-app purchases

Make a Noise

by Shiny Learning

http://www.shinylearning.co.uk/apps/index.shtml

- Includes switch access
- Android
- $2.26

Make It Pop
by Tryangle Labs
http://tryanglelabs.com/portfolio/make-it-pop
- iOS
- $1.99

Matching Puzzles for Kids
by Judy Lynn Software
http://www.judylynn.com/ipad
- iOS
- Free, in-app purchases available

Music Color
by SoundTouch
http://www.soundtouchinteractive.com/musiccolor
- iOS
- $4.99

Music Sparkles
by Kids Games Club
http://kidsgamesclubhouse.com
- iOS
- Free

Peekaboo Barn
by Night and Day Studios
http://www.nightanddaystudios.com/app/peekaboo-barn
- Android and iOS
- $1.99

Pocket Pond
by TriggerWave
http://www.triggerwave.com
- Android and iOS
- Free

Random Touch
by Joe Scrivens
https://sites.google.com/site/joescrivens/randomtouch
- iOS
- $.99

Ratatap Drums
by mode of expression
http://ratatapdrums.com
- iOS
- Free

Xylophone
by Piikea St.
http://www.piikeastreet.com/apps/xylophone
- iOS
- Free

ONLINE RESOURCES TO HELP
TEACH CAUSE AND EFFECT

There are many products that can be used to promote cause-and-effect responses in addition to mobile device apps. I have highlighted here some of my favorite developers of these products. Please refer to their websites for more information.

Don Johnston
http://www.donjohnston.com/products/low_incidence/c_e_software
- This company offers a variety of software such as Press-to-Play, Cause and Effect Cinema, and Attention Getter/Attention Teens.
- Mac and Windows
- Prices vary from about $30–$80

Helpkidzlearn
http://www.helpkidzlearn.com
- A collection of software for young children and those with learning difficulties to play online.
- The software can be played just using the space bar or a few other keys, and it can be used with special switches.
- Free

Hiyah.net
http://hiyah.net
- This company offers online software with a full variety of switch activities for learners with multiple or significant special needs.

- The activities listed are chosen because they can be used with switches, are simple, and don't require downloads.
- Free

Judy Lynn Software
http://www.judylynn.com

- This company offers a number of apps and downloadable programs to work on cause and effect and switch access.
- This company also produces some apps.

Northern Grid for Learning
http://northerngrid.org

- SENSwitcher consists of programs designed to help people with profound and multiple learning difficulties, those who need to develop skills with assistive input devices, and very young children new to computers.
- The program can be run directly from the website or downloaded for use on stand-alone PC or Macintosh computers.
- It includes 132 high-quality animated activities that can be operated by a wide range of input devices.
- Free

Shiny Learning
http://www.shinylearning.co.uk

- This company offers simple games that work on cause and effect, visual perception, and switch use.
- Many programs can be edited, allowing you to create your own tailored activities.
- There are free games online and software available for purchase.

CHAPTER 13

INTERACTIVE WEBSITES AND GAMES TO PROMOTE COMMUNICATION, LITERACY, AND LEARNING

Many people believe that playing games is a waste of time. This could not be further from the truth. Traditional and computer-based games are often goldmines in terms of helping people to improve reading, writing, speaking, understanding, and cognitive skills. It is often hard to distinguish between interactive multimedia sites designed for therapy and education and games for leisure and recreation. Board games, card games, strategy games, word games, and even games of luck, when used appropriately, offer enormous benefits. Children may be more easily engaged in activities and practice new skills without realizing that there is an educational process taking place. Brain research shows that brain pathways improve with practice. It's helpful if we can find ways for students with communication and cognitive challenges to practice the skills they are working on with enjoyable activities. Games can be effective tools for people with both severe and subtle deficits. Rules and activities often need to be modified to make them appropriate for each person. This can be accomplished by exploring and selecting options that are provided with the game and by varying the amount of assistance provided during the game.

As with other types of assistive technology, keep in mind the person's goals, visual impairments, fine motor abilities, cognitive and communication strengths and weaknesses, and interests.

RESOURCES FOR ADAPTED GAMES

Some people may benefit from products that were created to make games easier to play for people with disabilities. Products may be made larger and easier to manipulate. There are also games that were produced to be used to improve communication and cognition. Please refer to the following listings for more information.

- **Autism Games** (http://sites.google.com/site/autismgames), a collection of games with strong social components designed to be used with children with autism, with multiple levels of difficulty and suggested goals
- **Nanogames** (http://www.arcess.com), 30 fun, adapted games
- **RJ Cooper and Associates** (http://www.rjcooper.com), game controllers
- **Audiogames.net** (http://www.audiogames.net), games for the visually impaired
- **All in Play** (http://www.allinplay.com), some multiplayer games are fully accessible and were designed to work with a screen reader or screen magnifier

NEW EDUCATIONAL GAMING TECHNOLOGIES

Cell phones, iPods, iPads, Playstations, Wiis, Nintendo, Xbox, DSIs, computers, and other devices for playing games have become commonplace. A few of them lend themselves particularly well to helping people who have communication and cognitive challenges.

There are helpful games which come already installed on many computers. They can be used to work to improve attention, concentration, thinking, and use of the mouse or other selection method. For PCs, go to the Start Menu, then Programs, then Games. For Macs, go to http://www.apple.com/downloads.

These sites may be helpful when searching for mainstream games:
- **Amazon** (http://www.amazon.com)
- **Best Buy** (http://www.bestbuy.com)
- **Children's Software Online** (http://www.childrenssoftwareonline.com)
- **Board Game Central** (http://boardgamecentral.com)
- **Knowledge Adventure** (http://www.knowledgeadventure.com)
- **Smart Kids Software** (http://www.smartkidssoftware.com)
- **GameStop** (http://www.gamestop.com)

INTERACTIVE WEBSITES

Many of the following online resources do not require membership or fees. Some require logins and passwords. They may require Macromedia Shockwave or a Java platform—both of which can be downloaded at no charge. All should work on Mac and Windows devices; some may also work on iOS and Android devices, or may require an app. Clinicians and educators can adapt them all to work toward goals. Spend a bit of time checking out the sites to determine which are best and how they should be used. They can provide hundreds of hours of practice working on reading, writing, communication, and learning goals.

Below is a brief description of websites that are helpful for people with communication and learning challenges.

ABCMouse.com®
http://www.abcmouse.com
- This "Early Learning Academy" offers an extensive online curriculum for preschool and kindergarten.
- $7.95 per month

ABCYA.com
http://www.abcya.com
- This is a website with educational games and activities for elementary age students. Lessons are organized by grade level.
- Free

Brainpop
http://www.brainpop.com
- This website includes engaging animated movies and hundreds of standards-aligned quizzes, games, high-interest readings, and activities that cover lessons related to many academic subjects such as science, social studies, English, and math.
- $9.95 per month for family access
- Many different versions and pricing options are available.

CBeebies
http://www.bbc.co.uk/cbeebies
- CBeebies Online has many preschool characters and lots of fun games, stories, and activities. The activities develop computer skills and hand-eye coordination.
- Free

Children's Storybooks Online

http://www.magickeys.com/books

- Talking eBooks are provided with pictures categorized for young children, older children, and young adults. Online jigsaw puzzles, riddles, and games.
- Free

Discovery Education Brain Boosters

http://school.discoveryeducation.com/brainboosters

- This website offers a categorized archive of challenging Brain Boosters. Its activities work to improve categorizations, lateral thinking, logic, number and math play, reasoning, spatial awareness, and word and letter play.
- Free

Funbrain

http://www.funbrain.com

- This website has math, spelling, and creative writing games.
- Free

Gamequarium

http://www.gamequarium.com

- This website offers more than 1,500 links to online games that are categorized by core content. Kids can practice skills with scores and times to record on learning logs.
- Language arts activities include word fun, vocabulary games, parts of speech, sentence structure, spelling, and punctuation.
- Free

Goodwill Community Foundation International

http://www.gcflearnfree.org

- Gcflearnfree.org is an interactive website designed to help teach functional skills through a variety of online activities.
- There are different categories of learning available: Everyday Life, Math and Money, Computer Training, Online Classes, and Work and Career.
- The website is clean and easy to navigate.
- Signing up and using the resource is simple. Accessibility options are offered, as is a Spanish version.
- Free

Hiyah.net

http://www.hiyah.net

- This website offers software for children who need cause-effect programs. The programs are based on high-interest subjects, such as nursery rhymes, holidays, and birthday themes, and operate by pressing the spacebar.
- Free

Jigzone

http://www.jigzone.com

- This is a great website for puzzles with a wide variety of levels. You can determine the pictures, number of pieces, and shape.
- Free

Juniors Web

http://www.juniorsweb.com

- This website offers games to work toward speech therapy goals of speech, language, and literacy.
- Free

LanguageGuide.org

http://www.languageguide.org/english

- This is a website for learning vocabulary and grammar.
- Free

LearningPlanet.com

http://www.learningplanet.com

- LearningPlanet.com provides a wide variety of fun learning activities, educational games, printable worksheets, and powerful tools. Users can choose a grade level and get a list of games designed to improve the students' learning skills and proficiency in many different subjects.
- Free

ManyThings.org

http://www.manythings.org

- This website includes quizzes, word games, word puzzles, proverbs, slang expressions, anagrams, a random-sentence generator, and other computer-assisted language learning activities.
- Free

MrNussbaum.com

http://mrnussbaum.com

- This website includes many educational activities that help improve math, science, language arts, and social studies skills.
- Many of the games are customizable.
- Free

National Geographic Kids

http://www.kids.nationalgeographic.com

- This website has beautiful graphics, games, puzzles, coloring books, and other interactive activities.
- Free

ParentPals Special Education Games

http://www.parentpals.com/gossamer/pages/Special_Education_Games/index.html

- ParentPals offers a wide variety of Internet educational and therapy games, organized in levels of difficulty, to enhance learning and language skills.
- Free

PBS Kids

http://www.pbskids.org

- This website features many games and learning activities related to PBS shows such as Super Why!, WordWorld, and Little Pim.
- Free

Primary Games

http://www.primarygames.com

- This website offers interactive online games for elementary-age children.
- Free

Scholastic

http://www.scholastic.com

- This website offers games and activities for kids; activities, information, and advice for parents; lessons, activities, and tools for teachers; and trends, products, and solutions for administrators.
- Free

Sheppard Software

http://www.sheppardsoftware.com

- This website offers hundreds of games to learn about categories such as the USA, the world, animals, language arts, health, science, math, preschool, and the brain.
- There is a special section featuring top game choices for young children. Toward the bottom of the initial screen the programs are sorted for age groups, including preschool and kindergarten, elementary and early middle school, middle school and high school, and college and adults.
- Free

Smarty Games

http://www.smartygames.com

- This is a group of games for young children. If a child can move an on-screen pointer by mouse, joystick, touch window, trackball, voice or head pointer, he or she can play these simple games such as dot-to-dots, puzzles, telling time, coloring pictures, and more.
- Free

Starfall

http://www.starfall.com

- This is an elementary-level website for phonetic spelling and learning to read.
- There are more than 20 interactive stories with a variety of tasks for the emergent reader.
- It is phonics-based and requires the child to be able to click and drag.
- Free

Vizzle

http://www.monarchteachtech.com

- This is an online software tool used to help students with disabilities access the curriculum with multiple visual supports. There are more than 15,000 pieces of educator-approved audio, video, photo, and line drawing media built in and all lessons are customizable to meet the needs of the student.
- Contact company for pricing.

Vocabulary Building Games

http://www.vocabulary.co.il

- This website offers many easy-to-use crosswords, word search, hangman, jumbles, and matching games.
- Each activity has three levels of difficulty and provides a wide variety of topics.
- Free

VocabularySpellingCity.com

http://www.spellingcity.com

- There is a series of printable online games using a customizable spelling and vocabulary list.
- Individuals can enter five–10 spelling words, and Spelling City will turn this list into a word search, a matching game, hang mouse, crossword puzzle, and many more.
- There is a fee for the premium version.
- Free

ZacBrowser.com

http://zacbrowser.com

- This is an incredibly great website for young children and kids on the spectrum. There are many games and activities in this specialized browser appropriate for kids who have social, communication, and cognitive challenges.
- Free

CHAPTER 14

HELPFUL ONLINE RESOURCES AND LEARNING TOOLS

The web is full of valuable information. It has changed the way that we find and present information. The use of technologies such as the Internet as teaching tools in schools is now commonplace. Podcasts, instant messaging, text messages, and social networking sites have become mainstream, but individuals with communication, learning, and cognitive challenges often do not know how to take advantage of these new communication and learning tools.

Individuals who struggle with reading, writing, thinking, and speaking can benefit greatly from the access to information and communication the Internet offers, but are often not exposed to it. Hopefully, many of the assistive technologies presented in this guide will help solve that issue. If speaking is difficult, perhaps the student can type or send pictures online to express him- or herself, or communicate with live video to benefit from nonverbal communications. If reading is difficult, perhaps podcasts or use of text-to-speech tools would be a more appropriate way to gather information so that the student can listen rather than read. Social networking sites and Twitter can help people connect with others they may not be able to see in person. This chapter contains a brief description of some technology tools that are currently available with helpful examples of each, as well as some of my favorite sites to help search for apps.

APP SEARCH SITES

There is an increasing number of websites that can help with mobile app selection. Some offer video reviews, while others have created rubrics to assist with narrowing down the best apps for your purpose. Here are some that you may find helpful.

- **Bridging Apps** (http://bridgingapps.org), helps search for apps based on individual needs
- **Common Sense Media** (http://www.commonsensemedia.org), apps arranged by challenge area and difficulty level
- **Apps 4 Stages** (http://apps4stages.wikispaces.com), uses the Developmental Milestone Approach
- **Educational Technology and Mobile Learning** (http://www.educatorstechnology.com)
- **Apps for Children With Special Needs** (http://a4cwsn.com), app review videos
- **Spectronics Blog** (http://www.spectronicsinoz.com/apps-for-special-education), apps for special education

BLOGS

A blog is a web page made up of short, frequently updated postings that are arranged chronologically.

- **Twice Exceptional Blog** (http://2enewsletter.blogspot.com)
- **Teaching Learners with Multiple Special Needs** (http://teachinglearnerswithmultipleneeds.blogspot.com)
- **Special Education Law Blog** (http://specialeducationlawblog.blogspot.com)

DISCUSSION GROUPS, LISTSERVS, ELECTRONIC MAILING LISTS, AND BULLETIN BOARDS

Discussion groups or lists allow for ongoing discussions among members. They facilitate interaction among people because they enable members to post questions, comments, suggestions, or answers to a large number of users without everyone being available at the same time.

- Some are moderated, while others automatically accept all postings.
- They are typically fully or partially automated through the use of special mailing list software. Some mailing lists archive their postings, and these archives are available on the Internet for browsing.

- Some mailing lists are open to anyone who wants to join them, while others require an approval from the list owner in order for someone to join.
- Some are free; others require a fee.

Here are some examples:
- **Children's Disability Lists of Lists** (http://www.comeunity.com/disability/speclists.html)
- **University of Maryland, Disability-Related Listserves and Chatrooms** (http://www.inform.umd.edu/EdRes/Topic/Diversity/Specific/Disability/Listservs)
- **Commonwealth Center of Excellence in Stroke** (http://www.mc.uky.edu/stroke/Stroke-L.htm)
- **110 Online Special Education Graduate Programs** (http://www.gradschools.com/search-programs/online-programs/special-education)
- **TWIST at a Distance** (http://www.innovativespeech.com)

PODCASTS

A podcast is like an Internet radio show that you can download and listen to at your convenience, or listen to directly from the web. The majority of podcasts are MP3 files, which means that a person can listen to them on any MP3 player or on a computer. You can download one of any number of free software programs to your computer such as iTunes. The programs can be programmed to capture particular podcasts.

For a feel for what podcasts are like, check out these links:
- **LD Podcast** (http://www.ldpodcast.com)
- **John's Hopkins Medicine Podcasts** (http://www.hopkinsmedicine.org/mediaII/Podcasts.html)
- **Disability 411** (http://disability411.jinkle.com)
- **Prufrock Press Podcast** (http://blog.prufrock.com/gifted-education-podcast/)

RSS FEEDS

RSS feeds help connect web authors and their audience. Authors can choose to notify others automatically of new entries or changes to part of a website or blog by creating a feed. Others may choose to be notified automatically of those new entries or changes by subscribing to feeds.

Choosing to receive notification is called "subscribing" to the feed for that part of that website. Along with notification, the subscriber usually gets some form of direct access to the new or changed material.

New browsers have built-in feed detection, subscription, and management. An example can be found at CNN's website (http://www.cnn.com), which will send out headline news.

SCREEN SHARING OR DESKTOP SHARING, WEBINARS, ONLINE MEETINGS

You can share your computer screen in real-time so that everyone sees what you see—regardless of the application, software, or operating system you are using. This allows users to access any remote computer via Internet, just like sitting in front of it. This is often used during video/web conferences.

Programs differ in the number of people who can participate, whether or not people need to download software to participate, and the ability to record the sessions. Some programs have the capability to have participants join using smartphones. Most offer real-time collaboration with whiteboards and annotation tools, mouse and keyboard sharing, and instantly changing presenters. The following are free for individual use:

- **Mikogo** (http://www.mikogo.com)
- **Skype** (http://www.skype.com)

The following are paid for business use and have more attendees and features:

- **Adobe Connect** (http://www.adobeconnect.com)
- **Go to Meeting** (http://www.gotomeeting.com)

SOCIAL NETWORKING SITES

Social networking sites allow people to create profiles about themselves and connect or network with other people's profiles. Once they have networked with a friend, they can then see parts of the profiles of their friend's friends. As they connect with more and more people, their social network expands. These networks can then be used for fun, for connecting specific groups, and for arranging activities.

Some popular social networking sites include Facebook.com, and LinkedIn.com. Not as well known are the social networking sites created specifically to serve patients and families facing health challenges or who have individuals who need more "protected" sites.

- -

Caring Bridge
http://www.caringbridge.org
- A customized website can be created so that family and friends can be kept abreast of the patient's progress through the patient care journal and photo gallery, and can post words of encouragement through the guestbook.
- This program benefits the patient and family alike by keeping concerned loved ones informed of the patient's condition without the need for multiple phone calls or e-mails. It also creates a support group for the patient.
- Free

TEXT MESSAGING

Text messaging is a communication mode that allows users to exchange short messages through cell phones or other devices. It is especially helpful when talking on the phone is inappropriate or inconvenient and you want to communicate in real time.

Young people often would rather send text messages, post messages on social sites, and send instant messages than call someone on the phone or send an e-mail to communicate.

VIDEO CHAT

A video chat or video conference is a set of interactive telecommunication technologies that allows two or more locations to interact via two-way video and audio at the same time. For people with communication and cognitive challenges, video conferencing is a great way to communicate because nonverbal communication can augment verbal messages. It's really helpful to see the person with whom you are communicating. Some programs require downloads, but others don't. A webcam is needed to capture video. Without a webcam, users can still speak to each other—they just won't see each other. The following are free services (some offer paid premium options):
- **Google Hangout** (http://www.google.com/hangouts)

- **Skype** (http://skype.com)
- **ooVoo** (http://www.oovoo.com)

VIDEO ON THE WEB

Streaming media is a technology that delivers audio, video, images, and text to the user without downloading the entire file. It feeds the user only the portion of the file he or she needs at the moment.

- **YouTube** (http://www.youtube.com) offers users the opportunity at no cost to broadcast videos on the Internet. The video can be uploaded, tagged, and shared. It can also be used to view thousands of original videos that were uploaded by community members. There are many video groups to connect people of similar interests.
- **Atomic Learning** (http://www.atomiclearning.com) provides web-based training for assistive technology software and a few hardware devices. The training consists of short videos and demonstrations on how to use specific products. There are some free tutorials. A subscription fee is required to view the video tutorials based on use. Some offer closed captioning as an option.
- **Edublogs** (http://www.Edublogs.tv) is an example of a video blog to promote education. There is a great deal of video and audio for parents or teachers who want to explore more information on a variety of topics.

VIDEO PODCASTS

This term is used when video is provided on demand. For a great example, check out Closing The Gap—Assistive Technology Resources For Children and Adults With Special Needs (http://www.podcast.tv/video-podcasts/closing-the-gap-assistive-technology-resources-for-children-and-adults-with-special-needs-144726.html).

VISUALLY BASED CURRICULUM

Vizzle

http://www.monarchteachtech.com

- This is an online software tool used to help students with disabilities access the curriculum with multiple visual supports. There are more than 15,000 pieces of educator-approved audio, video, photo, and line drawing media built in and all lessons are customizable to meet the needs of the student.

- Contact company for pricing.

Web 2.0

http://www.go2web20.net

- This website is associated with applications that facilitate interactive information sharing and collaboration when online.

WEBSITES

Some websites require a subscription to some or all of the contents while others offer open access. Some subscriptions are free and some require a fee.

An example of a helpful website is Parents Helping Parents (http://www.php.com). It provides a great deal of very helpful information about parenting children with disabilities. There is a large amount of information about early intervention, identification, appropriate education, and support for parenting.

Website accessibility is becoming more important as Internet access becomes mainstream and more people with disabilities are learning to use assistive technology to obtain information and interact with online society. In the U.S., it is now the law that federally funded websites must be Section 508 Compliant, or accessible to those with disabilities. More information on this law can be found at http://www.section508.gov. For more information about accessibility issues, check out http://www.w3.org/WAI.

WIKIS

A wiki is a collaborative website comprised of the collective work of many authors. It allows users to easily upload, edit, and interlink pages. The most popular and well-known wiki is Wikipedia (http://www.wikipedia.com), an open content encyclopedia. It is offered in many languages. The UDL Tech Toolkit (http://udltechtoolkit.wikispaces.com) by assistive and educational technology consultant Karen Janowski is a great wiki about assistive technology for students.

REFERENCES

· · · · · · · · · · · · · ·

Assistive Technology Act of 2004, 4278 H.R. § 3.4 (2004). In www. GovTrack.us. Retrieved from http://www.govtrack.us/congress/bills/ 108/hr4278

Kurzweil Educational Systems (n.d.). Kurzweil 3000 supports Universal Design for Learning. Retrieved from http://www.kurzweiledu.com/ files/Kurzweil%203000%20and%20UDL.pdf

ABOUT THE AUTHOR

· · · · · · · · · · · ·

Joan L. Green, founder of Innovative Speech Therapy, is a speech-language pathologist in the Washington, DC, area with many years of experience helping children as well as adults who have a wide range of communication, cognitive, literacy, and learning challenges. She provides unique cutting-edge therapy, consultation, and training for families and professionals. Joan is passionate in her efforts to spread the word about how affordable state-of-the-art technology can be used to empower children and adults who experience difficulty with speaking, reading, writing, thinking, understanding, and learning at home, school, work, or in the community.

She authored *Technology for Communication and Cognitive Treatment: The Clinician's Guide*, which was published in 2007, as well as the first edition of this book, which was published in 2011. Joan received the Most Outstanding Contribution to the Field Award from the Maryland Speech-Language Hearing Association in 2008. She received her professional training at Northwestern University and is the mother of four wonderful children.

Joan offers live and recorded webinars as well as an informative free e-newsletter, "Innovative Technology Treatment Solutions," that highlights technology treasures and effective strategies for professionals and families to help maximize progress toward goals. A listing of her therapy programs, description of her books, and information about her presentations as well as services can be found at http://www.innovativespeech.com.

INDEX

. . . .

@Reks, 196
+Sudoku, 205

123s ABCs Handwriting Fun, 152
4 in a Row Online, 195
8interactive Limited, 106
22Learn, 118
24 x 7 digital, 120
2Do Tasks Done in Style, 172
77Sparx Studio, 199
84 Logic Games, 195
110 Online Special Education Graduate
    Programs, 223

AAC Evaluation Genie, 13
AAC Institute, 64
AAC Language Lab, 64
AAC TechConnect, 64
ABA Flashcards- Actions, 44
ABA Receptive, 79
ABA—Which Does Not Belong?, 195
Abby Sight Word Games & Flash Cards,
    118
Abbyy, 94
ABC Alphabet Phonics, 118
ABC Phonics Word Family, 118
ABC Pocket Phonics, 118
ABCMouse.com, 106, 215
ABCya.com, 121, 215
Abilipad, 132
AbilityNet GATE, 23
AbilityHub, 23, 24
Abitalk, 118, 123, 158
AbleLink Technologies, 174
AbleNet, 67, 69, 85
Absurd, 54
Academic Earth, 187
Accessible Book Collection, 99
Adobe Connect, 224
Aesop's Quest, 122
Age of Learning, 106
Alexicom Tech, 70
All in Play, 214
all4mychild, 52, 56
Alphabet, Spelling and Phonics!, 154
Amazon, 104, 154, 199, 214
American Speech-Language Hearing
    Association, 27

Andrea Sabbatini, 195
Andrew Sulimoff, 137
Angela Reed, 122
AnimalBrainz, 183
Animal Hide & Seek Adventure, 195
Annenberg Learner, 188
Answers:YesNo, 68
AnyBook Anywhere, 107
Anymeeting, 184
Apple Accessibility, 24
Apps 4 Stages, 222
Apps for Children with Special Needs,
    222
Apps in My Pocket, 118
Apraxia-KIDS, 27
Apraxia Picture Sound Cards, 32
Apraxia Ville, 32
ARTEFACT, 41
Articulate it!, 33
Articulation Flip Books, 33
Articulation Games, 33
Articulation Scenes, 33
Articulation Station, 34
ArtikPix- Full, 34
Assessing Students' Needs for Assistive
    Technology, 13
Assistive Apps, 70, 132
Assistive Express, 70, 132
Assistive Listening Device Systems, 85
AssistiveTech.net, 24
AssistiveWare, 72, 103, 141, 187
ATEval2Go, 13
Atomic Learning, 226
Attainment Company, 67, 68
Audible, 105
Audio Note, 183
Audiobooks, 97, 101, 104, 105, 107
Audiogames.net, 214
Auditory Analysis, 119
Auditory Processing Studio, 79, 80
Auditory Workout, 80, 195
Autism Games, 214
Autism Language Learning, 47, 48, 50, 52
Autismate, 70, 187
Avaz for Autism, 71
Awesome Note, 172
Awesome Giant, 195

Baby Bus, 202
Bacciz, 106
Baek Pack, 95
Balabolka, 93
Balloon Bang, 208
Barbara Fernandes, 27, 207
Basic Sequencing Skills, 195
BBC Languages, 57
BBC Schools, 159
Bejeweled, 196
Bejoy Mobile, 209
Ben Kaiser, 156
Best Buy, 214
Between the Lions, 110
BigIQkids, 154
BigIQkids Spelling Program, 154
Big Bang Patterns, 208
Big Think, 188
BIGTrack, 21
Binary Labs, 120
Bing, 3
Bitsboard, 79
Bla Bla Bla, 40, 208
Blackberry, 34, 101, 119, 209
Blockdot, 154
Blue Tags, 173
Blue Whale, 39
Board Game Central, 214
Bob Books, 119
Boggle, 196
Bookabi, 142
BookBox, 104
Bookshare, 95, 98, 105
Boreaal, 153
Brain Boosters, 193, 216
BrainHQ, 193
Brainpop, 82, 188, 215
BrainPro, 110
BrainTrain Memory Gym PE, 192
Branchfire, 135
Brian Stokes, 41
Bridging Apps, 222
Bridworks, 172
brightstorm, 188
Browser Books, 99
Brush of Truth, 106
Bubbl.us, 145
Building Thinking Skills, 192
Byki (Before you know it), 57

Caboose Express: Patterns and Sorting, 196

Calendars+, 173
CalenMob, 173
Capture Notes 2, 140
Caring Bridge, 225
Caroline Bowen, 43
Carolyn LoGuidice, 157
Category Carousel, 196
Categories Learning Center, 196
Category TherAppy, 196
Cause and Effect Cinema, 211
Cause and Effect Sensory Light Box, 208
CBeebies, 215
Center for Applied Special Technology, 6
CHADD, 162
Charge Your Brain, HD, 194
Checkers Free, 197
Checkmark, 168
Cheryl Bregman, 132
Chicktionary for iPad, 154
Child Development Game Suite, 197
Children's Disability Lists of Lists, 223
Children's Software Online, 214
Children's Storybooks Online, 216
Choice Board Creator, 174
Chromebook, 16, 19
Cindy Meester, 27
Classroom Complete Press, 158
Classroom Suite, 95
Clean Up: Category Sorting, 197
Clear Sky Apps, 140
Clever Fox, 195, 197
Click N Kids, 110
Click N Read Phonics, 110
Clicker, 97, 99, 144
Clicker Docs, 132, 139
Clicker Sentences, 144
Clicky Sticky, 54
Closing the Gap, 226
CNN, 224
Co:Writer, 139
Co-writer, 133
Cognable, 208
Cognitive Concepts, 110
Cognitopia Software, 170
Collaborative for Communication Access via Captioning, 86
Color Dots, 208
Common Core State Standards, 6, 139
Common Sense Media, 222
Commonwealth Center of Excellence in Stroke, 223
Communicate: Symwriter, 97

Compass Access Assessment Software, 13
Complete Class Organizer, 183
Comprehension TherAppy, 80
Connor Zwick, 176
Consumer Reports, 16
Conversation, 83
ConversationBuilderTeen, 55
Conversation Cards, 54
Conversation Paceboard, 40
Conversation TherAppy, 54
Cookie Doodle, 55, 197
Cosmeo, 188
Course Hero, 176
Crack the Books iTextbooks, 100
Cram, 176
Crick Software, 97, 132, 134, 139, 144, 152
Critical Thinking Company, The, 115, 192
Cross Forward Consulting, 105
Crossword Adventure for Kids, 155
Cubic Frog Apps, 203
CurriculaWorks, 111
Custom Boards Premium, 66
Custom Solutions, 159
Custom Typing Training, 159
Cut the Rope, 197

DAF Assistant, 41
Dance Mat Typing, 159
David Estes, 183
Describe It, 44, 81
Describe It to Me, 44
Describe With Art, 82
Described and Captioned Media Program, 86
Developing Critical Thinking Skills Online, 114
Diane German, 43
Different Roads to Learning, 197
Digital Storytime, 106
Diigo, 179
Disability 411, 223
Discovery Education, 193, 216
Disney, 106
Doceri, 178
Dolphin Reader, 91
Don Johnston, 14, 96, 101, 133, 138, 152, 159, 181, 211
Doodle Buddy, 197
Doonan Speech Therapy, 39, 48, 49, 51, 204
Dots- Online, 197
Draft:Builder, 139

Dragon Apps, 34
Dragon Dictate, 148
Dragon Dictation, 23, 34, 148
Dragon Dictation Mobile Apps, 148
Dragon NaturallySpeaking, 147, 148
Drillaby Pro, 35
Droid Spell Kids, 155
Doist, 171
Dropbox, 6, 68, 94, 95, 132, 135, 139, 175, 182
Duck Duck Moose, 206
Duolingo, 57
Dynavox Mayer-Johnson, 24, 67, 97

Earobics, 110
EasyConcepts, 81, 198
Easy Speak Enterprises, 81, 198
Easy World of English, 84
Editor in Chief Software, 156
Edmark, 111
Edublogs, 226
Educational Technology and Mobile Learning, 222
Educreations, 178
Educreations Interactive Whiteboard, 178
Electric Eggplant, 106
Electronic Arts, 196
Ellie's Games, 208
Enablemart, 22, 24, 91, 111
Enabling Devices, 67
English Adventures for Kids, 83
EnglishClub Listening, 84
Eric Sailers, 27, 107, 123
Errands To-Do List, 173
ESOL Courses, 85
Evernote, 6, 95, 135, 136, 139, 141, 148, 149, 168, 179, 182
Expedition With Plurals, 50
Expert Software Applications, 146
Explain Everything, 178
Explode the Code® Online, 111
Expressive Solutions, 34, 36, 123
Express SLP, 35

Face Changer, 83
Facebook, 27, 40, 72, 105, 173, 184, 204, 224
Facetime, 85, 187
Fast ForWord, 110, 111
Fido's Magic Soundbox, 78
Find My iPhone, 74
Find the Differences, 198

Finger Paint with Sounds, 209
Firefly, 137
Fireworks Games, 209
First Author Writing Software, 159
First Phrases, 35, 47, 48, 157
First Then Visual Schedule, 169
First Words Deluxe, 119, 155
Fit Brains Trainer, 194
Fizzbrain, 153
Flashcard Machine, 176
Flashcard Machine Mobile, 176
Flashcards+, 176
Flashcards++, 176
FoxVox, 93
Foundations Developmental House, 32
Foundation Mir, 199
Franklin Electronic Publishers, 107
Freedom Scientific, 94, 96, 139, 181
Freefall Spelling, 155
Fun With Directions, 81, 198
Funbrain, 216
Functional Conversation, 55
Fundación Planeta Imaginario, 198

G8R Software, 140
Galaxy Tablet, 20
Gamequarium, 216
Gcflearnfree.org, 112, 216
gdiplus, 153
Ghotit, 133, 134, 138
Ginger Labs, 140, 183
Ginger Software, 133, 134
Glenda Anderson, 27
Glogster, 141, 233
Glogster Edu, 141
Go Read, 98
Go to Meeting, 224
Good Karma Applications, 69, 169, 172
Good Neighbor Press, 203
Good.iWare, 135
Goodwill Community Foundation
    International, 112, 216
Google+, 74, 184, 185
Google Calendar, 169
Google Chromebook, 16, 19
Google Chrome-Speakit!, 93
Google Docs, 129, 137
Google Drive, 95, 135, 140, 175, 177, 182, 185
Google Hangout, 74, 85, 185, 225
Google Tasks, 171
GoTalk, 67, 68

Grammar Checker, 133, 134
Grammar Fitness Online, 157
Grammar Jammers, 157
GrammarPrep, 157
GrasshopperApps.com, 36, 48, 53, 79, 80, 118, 142, 158, 187, 199, 205
Grembe, 45
GridPlayer, 71
Guess the Code, 198
Guess the Person?, 198
Guided Ways Technologies, 172
gFlash+ Flashcards & Tests, 177
gWhiz, 177

Haiku Deck, 141
Hamaguchi Apps, 35, 47, 48, 56, 81, 157, 198
Handhold Adaptive, 42, 169, 174
Handwriting Without Tears, 127
Handy Apps, 171
Harmony Applications, 200
Harris Communications, 85
Haywoodsoft, 143
HeadSprout, 114
Heads Up, 44
Hear Builder®: Following Directions, 84
HearBuilder Phonological Awareness, 112
HearBuilder Sequencing, 192
Hearing Loss Web, 85
HelpKidzLearn, 14, 211
Hiyah.net, 15, 211, 217
Hop, Skip and Jump, 112
Houghton Mifflin Harcourt, 106
How to Write a Paragraph, 158
Hippocampus.org, 188
Hump Software, 13

I Can Articulate, 35
I Get It, 174
I Like Stories, 53, 142
iAnnotate, 135
iBooks, 95, 99, 100
iCloud, 6, 99
IDC, 201
iLoveFireworks, 209
Inclusive Technology, 208, 209
Incorporate Apps, 171
Independent Living Aids, 91
Injini, 68, 153, 197, 209
Innovative Mobile Apps, 79, 120, 200
Innovative Net Learning, 157
Innovative Speech Therapy, 129, 231

Innovative Technology Treatment Solutions, 231
Inspiration Maps, 145
Inspiration Software, 145, 152, 181
Intellitools, 95
Intent Software, 199
Interactive Alphabet ABCs, 119
International Children's Digital Library, 100
International Dyslexia Association, The, 88
International Society for Augmentative and Alternative Communication, The, 65
Intersog, 173
Intuitive Innovations, 199
Invention Labs, 71
iPractice Verbs, 49
iPrompts, 169, 174
Is & Are Fun Deck, 49
isequences, 198
iSpotPro for Kids, 199
iStudiez Pro, 170
iTouchiLearnWords:Speech & Language Skills, 119
iTunes, 28, 100, 188, 223
iTurnStones, 199
iWordQ, 133, 135
iWriteWords, 153
iTeacherBook, 170

Janice Light, 65
Jason Lustig, 176
Jean-Eudes Lepelletier, 53, 187
Jigsaw Box, 199
Jigsaw Puzzles, 199, 216
Jigzone, 217
Joan L. Green, 27, 231
Joe Scrivens, 210
John Halloran, 53
John's Hopkins Medicine Podcasts, 223
Join.me, 184
Jonah Bonah Learning Company, The, 37
JotNot Scanner Pro, 136, 186
Joy Zabala, 12, 65
Judy Lynn Software, 14, 203, 210, 212
Jumbled Sentences, 157
Juniors Web, 217

Kachalo and Balashoff, 170
Kaleidoscope Drawing Pad, 209
Karen Janowski, 4, 227
Kathy Drager, 65

Khan Academy, 189
Kindle, 18, 101, 102, 104–106, 121
Kenneth Grisham, 94
KeyStageFun, 156
Kids ABC Phonics, 119
Kids Animal Toys (Real Sounds), 78
Kids Game Club, 202
Kids Memory Games, 199
Kids Puzzles, 199
Kids Puzzles Puzzingo, 199
Kids Reading Comprehension, 122
Kidspiration, 145
Kindergarten.com, 44, 79, 195
KneeBouncers, 209
Knowledge Adventure, 214
Koester Performance Research, 13
Kurzweil 3000, 94, 96, 137, 145, 181, 229
Kurzweil Educational Systems, 94, 96, 137, 181, 229

L'Escapadou, 153, 155
Lamp Words for Life, 71
Language Builder, 47
Language Empires, 121
Language Lab: Core Words, 47, 49
Language Lab: Directing Activities, 49
Language Lab: ing Verbs + Prepositions, 49
Language Lab: Plurals, 50
Language Learning Apps, 52
LanguageGuide.org, 217
Launch Pad, 138
Launchpad Toys, 143
Lauren Enders, 4, 146
LD OnLine, 89, 124, 127, 154, 162
LD Podcast, 223
LeapFrog, 107
LeapReader, 107
Learnbat, 178
Learn to Talk First Words- Preschool, Kindergarten Flash Cards, 45
LearnEnglish Kids, 57
Learning Ally, 98, 99
Learning Company, The, 114
Learning Paths, 65
Learning Touch, 119, 155
LearningPlanet.com, 217
Lenovo, 16
Lensoo, 178
Letter Reflex, 120
Let's Name . . . Things Fun Deck, 45
Let's Talk Apps, 81

Let's Talk Following Instructions, 81
LetterSchool, 153
Lexercise, 112
Lexia Learning Systems, 113
Lexia Reading Software, 113
Lexico Cognition, 81
Librivox, 100
LingualNet, 82
Linguisystems, 55, 84, 115, 116, 157
LinkedIn, 27, 224
Listening Master, 82
Literactive, 113
Literacy Productivity Pack, 96
Little Bee Speech, 34
Little Big Thinkers, 155
Little Solver, 200
Live Mocha, 57
LiveBinders, 179
LiveScribe, 67, 148, 149, 164, 181, 182, 234
LiveScribe Pen, 67, 148, 181, 182
Logan Technologies, 66
Logic Puzzles, 200
LogiGrid Logic Problem Puzzles, 200
LOGO-Start Publishers, 54
Lorraine Curran, 40
Lorenzo Bravi, 40, 208
Low Vision Gateway, The, 91
Luminant Software, 183
Lumos Labs, 193, 194
Lumosity.com, 164, 193, 194
Lumosity Mobile, 194

Mad Rabbit, 204
Magma Mobile, 200
Make a Noise, 209
Make It Pop, 210
Make My Face, 83
Making Sequences, 200
ManyThings.org, 217
Marbles the Brain Store, 192
Matching Puzzles for Kids, 210
MatchUp: Exercise Your Memory, 200
MathTV, 189
MatrixMatch 1, 200
Maverick Software, 201
Mayuir Sidhpara, 199
MeeGenius, 106
Memory Matches 2, 201
Memory Train, 201
Memory Trainer, 201
MemoryBlock, 200

MeMoves, 201
Merge Mobile, 54, 83, 143, 155
Merit Software, 113, 152, 157, 159
Michael Spade, 173
Microsoft Accessibility, 24
Microsoft Corporation, 138, 181
Microsoft Word, 13, 128, 129, 132, 138, 145, 181, 183
Microsoft Windows, 16, 18
Mikogo, 224
Mimio Home Reading Programs, 114
MimioSprout, 114
Mind Benders, 192
Mind inFormation, 112
Mind the Frog, 205
Mindex International, 94
MINDOMO, 146
Mindshapes, 106
Minimal Pairs Academy, 36
Mindspring Software, 192
MintLeaf Software, 41
Mobile Education Store, 47–49, 51, 52, 100, 121, 152, 158
Mobile OCR Free, 94, 137
MobiTech 3000, 136, 186
MobilityWare, 203
mode of expression, 211
Monkey Word School Adventure, 120
Montessori Crosswords, 155
Moofy Recognizing Pattern Games, 201
More Buffet!, 201
MorrisCooke, 178
Mozilla Firefox, 93
Mozzaz Corporation, 72
MrNussbaum.com, 218
Multimedia Speech Pathology, 39
Multiple Choice Articulation, 36
Multiple Meanings Library, 45
Music Color, 210
Music Sparkles, 202, 210
My First 1,000 Words, 120
My First AAC, 68
My Baby Gets Organized, 202
My Pictures Talk, 45
MyFirstApp, 200, 203
MyHomework Student Planner, 170
My Pictures Talk, 45
My PlayHome, 55, 83, 202
My Zoo Animals: Toddler's Seek & Find, 202
MyScript, 141, 149
MyScript Notes Mobile, 141

Naming TherAppy, 45
Nancy Inman, 144
Nanogames, 214
National Association of the Deaf, 86
National Center for Accessible Media, 86
National Center for Learning Disabilities, The, 88, 124, 162
National Geographic Kids, 218
National Institute of Child Health and Human Development, 89
National Institute of Mental Health, 162
National Institute of Neurological Disorders and Stroke, 162
National Institute on Deafness and Other Communication Disorders, 86
National Institutes of Health, 162
Natural Reader, 93
NaturalSoft, 93
NC Soft, 209
Nebulous Notes, 140
Neok12, 189
News-2-You, 103
NewsCurrents, 103
NextUp, 93
Night and Day Studios, 210
No-Glamour Grammar Interactive Software, 157
Nook, 101, 104, 105, 121
Northern Grid, 15, 212
Notability, 140, 183
Notes Plus, 140
Noun, 79
Now What, 170
NRCC Games, 122
Nth Fusion, 195
Nuance, 34, 136, 147, 148
Nuclear Elements, 140

Oceanhouse Media, 106
One Minute Reader, 123
One Step Two Step, 81, 202
Onion Mountain Technology, 127
Online Leveled Reading Library, 100, 116
Optime Software, 197, 198, 205
Overdrive Media Console, 101
ooVoo, 74, 185, 226

Pages, 128, 129, 138
Pandora Media, 202
Pandora Radio, 202
Pangaea Learning, 57
PaperPort Notes, 136

Pappy GMBH, 81
Parents Helping Parents, 227
Pass it On Center, 24
Paragraph Punch Online, 159
ParentPals Special Education Games, 218
PBS Kids, 110, 121, 218
PC Magazine, 16
Pearson Education, 157
Peekaboo Barn, 210
Penguin Leveled Readers, 106
Phonics Studio, 36
PhonoPix- Full, 36
Pictello, 141, 187
Picture Planner, 170
Picture the Sentence, 81
Picture Word Power, 144
Pi'ikea St., 119
Pine Cone Software, 198
Pinger, 197
Pinterest, 4, 27, 146
Pirate Pad, 185
Pixel Interactive, 78
PlayTales, 106
Pocket Artic, 37
Pocket Pairs, 37
Pocket Pond, 210
PositScience, 164, 193
Powerpoint, 13, 93, 142
PlaySmart-Kids, 156, 201
Plurality, 50
Plurals Fun Deck, 51
Practical Parenting, 127
Pre-Number Category Sorting Matching Game, 203
Predictable, 71
Premier Literacy, 93, 96, 135, 138, 181
Premier Talking Reader, 94
Prentke Romich Company, 47, 49, 50, 64, 71
Preposition Builder, 51
Preposition Remix, 51
Preschool EduKidsRoom, 203
Preschool University, 78, 120, 122
Press-to-Play, 211
Prezi, 142
Primary Games, 218
Project Gutenberg, 101
Proloquo2go, 72, 187
Pronoun Fill-in Super Fun Dec, 50
ProxTalker App, 66
Prufrock Press Podcast, 223
Punctuation Puzzler Software, 158

Puzzle Baron, 200
Pyxwise Software, 156

Questions2Learn, 52, 82
Question Builder, 52
QuestionIt, 52
Question Sleuth, 52
Quillsoft, 23, 133, 135, 148
Quizlet, 176, 177

R Intensive SLP, 37
Rainbow Sentences, 121
Randall's ESL Cyber Listening Lab, 84
Random Touch, 210
Ratatap Drums, 211
RAZ-Kids Online Leveled Reading
    Library, 100, 116
Read & Write, 134, 138, 145
Read and Write Desktop, 96
Read Naturally, 123
Read to Know, 103
Read:OutLoud, 96, 181
Read2Go, 98
Readability, 91
Readdle, 137, 173, 186
Reader Rabbit, 114
Reading Assistant, 114
Reading Champion, 123, 138
Reading Comprehension Booster Online,
    113
Reading Comprehension Camp, 123
Reading Comprehension for Kindergarten
    and First Grade, 123
Reading Comprehension Level 1
    Interactive Software, 115
Reading Comprehension Solar System for
    5th Grade, 123
Reading Detective Software, 115
Reading Rainbow, 106
Reading Remedy, 115
Readwritethink, 89
Real Writer & Reader, 134, 138
RehabMart, 22
RehabTool.com, 24
Remember the Milk, 171
Rhymezone, 43
Richard Buckingham, 198
Richard Humphrey, 170
RJ Cooper & Associates, 15, 22, 24
Rob Ellis, 155
Rocket Languages, 57
Rocket Reader, 116

Rocket Speller, 155
Rock n Learn, 120
Rodrigo Neri, 170
Rosetta Stone, 57
Route 66 Literacy, 116
RWH Technology, 38, 41

Samsung, 16
Scanner Pro, 137, 186
Scene Speak, 69
Schedule Planner, 173
Scholastic, 102, 117, 218
Scientific Learning, 110, 111, 114, 115
Scoompa, 83
Sean Sweeney, 27
Second Guess, 133
Sensory Software International, 71
SENSwitcher, 15, 212
Sentence Builder, 70, 122, 158
Sentence Maker, 48, 158
Sentence Reading Magic, 122
Sentence Workout, 158
SentenceBuilder, 158
Sequencing Tasks: Life Skills, 203
Serious Tree, 39
Set Enterprises, 203
Set Pro HD, 203
SETT Framework, The, 12, 65
Sheppard Software, 219
Shimon Young, 55, 202
Shiny Learning, 15, 208, 209, 212
Shoe the Goose, 55, 197
ShowMe Interactive Whiteboard, 178
Sierra Vista Software, 122
Sight Words for Reading, 120
Sight Words Sentence Builder, 122
SightWords Pro, 120
Silver Kite, 73, 187
Simple Student, 173
Simplex Spelling, 156
Simplified Touch, 68
Simply Find It Pro, 204
Simply Game, 204
Skill Builder Spelling, 156
Skitch, 136
Skype, 74, 85, 184, 185, 187, 224, 226
SlideIT, 147
SlowTunes, 41
SLP Tech Tools, 35
SmallPlanet, 106
Smart Kids Software, 214
Smart Kids With LD, 162

Smart Mobile Software, 94, 137
SmartScan + OCR: Text Reader with PDF Conversion, 137
Smarty Ears, 13, 32, 33, 36, 37, 44, 49, 51, 66, 121–123, 196, 207
Smarty Games, 219
Snowman, 168
SoftMaker Presentations Mobile, 142
Softmaker Software GMBH, 142
Softpedia, 93
Solitaire, 203
SOLO Literacy Suite, 96, 138
Sonneta Voice Monitor, 41
Sono Flex, 72
Sort It Out, 203
Sort This Out Pack, 204
Sound Beginnings, 78, 120
Sound Reading Solutions, 112, 115
Sounding Board, 69
SoundNote, 183
SoundTouch, 78, 210
SP Controls, 178
Spaced Retrieval, 204
Speak in Motion, 40, 206
SpeakQ, 23, 135, 148
SpecialNeedsWare, 70, 187
Spectronics, 65, 222
Speech Box for Speech Therapy, 37
Speech Cards Professional, 38, 41
Speech Flipbook, 38
Speech Pairs, 38
Speech Prompts, 42
Speech Pups, 52, 82
Speech Sounds on Cue for iPad, 39
Speech Stickers, 39
Speech Therapy for Apraxia- NACD, 39
Speech Tree, 72
Speech With Milo Articulation Board Game, 39
Speech With Milo: Prepositions, 51
Speech With Milo: Sequencing, 204
Speech With Milo Verbs, 48
SpeechPrompts, 42, 169
SpellingCity, 156, 220
Sparkle Apps, 199
Special Education Law, 222
Speech and Language Store, 204
Splashtop, 178
Splashtop Whiteboard, 178
Splingo's Language Universe, 204
Spotlight on Reading & Listening Comprehension Levels 1 and 2, 116

Spot the Differences, 204
Spoty Location Reminder, 171
Squeebles Spelling Test, 156
Starfall Education, 121
Start-to-Finish Online Accessible Library, 101
Staytoooned, 119
Storia, 102, 106, 117
Story Bayou, 106
Story Patch, 143
Storybird, 143
Storybook Maker, 143
StoryBuilder for iPad, 55
StoryPals, 107, 123
Storyline Online, 102
StoryMaker, 169
Study Stack, 176
Stuttering Foundation, 27
Sunburst, 160
Super Duper Publications, 45, 49–51, 112, 192
Super Note, 140
Super Why!, 121, 218
Swan Soft, 205
Switch in Time, 14
Swype, 147
SymbolStix, 66, 71, 72, 103
Symbaloo, 180
SymbalooEdu, 180
Synapse Apps, 37, 38, 44, 81, 196, 202
Sync.in, 185

Tactus Therapy Solutions, 38, 45, 54, 80, 196, 206
Talking Photo Albums, 67, 68
Talking Talk, 119
Talking Tiles, 72
Talking Train, 56
Talking Word Processor, 181
TalkTime Pediatric Speech Academy, 47, 48, 50, 52
Tamajii, 142
Tapikeo, 53, 187
Tap Speak Choice AAC, 73
TapSpeak Sequence, 69
Tar Heel Reader, 102
Tasks N Todos Pro, 171
TeachersParadise.com, 152
TeacherTube, 189
Teaching Learners with Multiple Special Needs, 222
TechMatrix, 89

Techno Chipmunk, 174
TED, 189
Ted Conley, 69, 73
Tense Builder, 48, 49
Text Help, 96, 134, 181
TextAloud3, 93
Therapro, 127
Therapy Box Limited, 71, 204
Things That Go Together, 205
Thinking Moves, 201
ThinkPad, 16
Thunderloop, 45
THUP Games, 120
Tic Tac Toe, 205
Time4Learning, 117
Tipirneni Software, 136
Titan Pad, 185
Tobii Technology, 72
Toca Boca AB, 56, 205
Toca Hair Salon 2, 56
Toca Kitchen, 205
Toddler Puzzle Woozzle, 205
Todoist, 171
Toontastic, 143
TopTenReviews, 148, 159
Touch and Write, 153
TouchChat, 73, 144, 187
Touch the Sound, 79
Tozzle, 205
Trans-code Design, 136
Tribal Nova, 154
TriggerWave, 210
Tryangle Labs, 210
Tumblebook Library, 103
Twice Exceptional, 222
TWIST at a Distance, 223
Type to Learn 4: Agents of Information, 160

UDL Tech Toolkit, 146, 227
Universal Reader Plus, 93
University of Maryland, Disability-Related Listserves and Chatrooms, 223
Unusual Things, 194, 196
Urbian, 201
Using I and Me Fun Deck, 50

VAST Autism 1- Core, 40
VAST Songs, 206
vBookz PDF Voice Reader US, 94
Verbal Reasoning, 56
VG Web Solutions, 155
Viet Tran, 140

Virtual Speech Center, 33, 45, 46, 50, 56, 79, 80, 82, 158, 195
Vision Objects, 141
Visual Attention TherAppy, 206
Visual Impact Pro, 174
Visual Schedule Planner, 172
Vivity Labs App, 194
Vizzle, 219, 226
Vocabulary Building Games, 220
VocabularySpellingCity.com, 220
Voice Dream, 95

Warner Bros., 44
Watchknowlearn.org, 189
Watchminder, 172
Web 2.0, 6, 227
Web Reader (TTS Web Browser), 95
Webspiration, 145
Wee Black Sheep Entertainment, 54
Weikuan Zhou, 204
What's in the bag?, 52
Wheels on the Bus, 206
WhQuestions, 51, 122
Wikipedia, 227
Windows 8, 16, 18, 28
Wisconsin Assistive Technology Initiative, 13
WireCloud, 83
Wonderkind Interaktionsmedien GmbH, 202
Word BINGO, 121
WordQ + Speak Q, 135
Word Retrieval, 46
Word Slapps Vocabulary, 80
WordToob, 53
Write My Name, 153
Write Now, 135
Write: OutLoud, 139
WriteOnline, 134, 139
Writing Wizard, 153
Wynn Literacy Software, 94
WYNN Reader, 96

XigXag Interactive, 78
Xylophone, 211

Yoctoville, 173
You're the Storyteller, 56
YouTube, 3, 24, 29, 165, 177, 189, 226

ZacBrowser.com, 220
Zeptolab, 197
Zorten Software, 50, 80, 200